P9-DUJ-689

IS FOR BABY

26 Projects from A to Z

Suzonne Stirling

Photographs by Mary Ellen Bartley

The Taunton Press
Inspiration for hands-on living®

Text © 2006 by Suzonne Stirling

Photographs © 2006 by Mary Ellen Bartley

Illustrations © 2006 by The Taunton Press, Inc.

All rights reserved.

The Taunton Press, Inc., 63 South Main Street, PO Box 5506, Newtown, CT 06470-5506
e-mail: tp@taunton.com

Editor: Julie Hamilton
Jacket/Cover design: 3+Co.
Interior design & layout: 3+Co.
Illustrator: Christine Erickson
Photographer: Mary Ellen Bartley

Library of Congress Cataloging-in-Publication Data
Stirling, Suzonne.
B is for baby : 26 projects from A to Z / Suzonne Stirling ; photographer : Mary Ellen Bartley.
   p. cm.
ISBN-13: 978-1-56158-854-1
ISBN-10: 1-56158-854-7
1. Handicraft. 2. Infants' supplies. 3. Children's paraphernalia. I. Title.
TT157.S755 2006
745.5--dc22

                          2006011155

Printed in China
10 9 8 7 6 5 4 3 2 1

The following manufacturers/names appearing in *B is for Baby* are trademarks: Anna Griffin™, Avery™, Beacon Adhesives®, Britex Fabrics®, Chatterbox Inc.®, Clipart.com℠, Create for Less℠, Dick Blick℠, eBay℠, EZ Crafts Pressure-fax®(transfer pen and paper), Fabri-Tac™, Fiskars®, Fray Check™, FrayBlock™, Glue Dots®, HeatnBond®, Impress® Rubber Stamps, IKEA℠, iTunes®, Jo-Ann Stores℠, Jupiterimages℠, Kate's Paperie℠, M&J Trimming℠, Magic Cabin Dolls℠, Making Memories®, Mod Podge®, Paper Source®, PEELnSTICK™, Perfect Glue™, Scotch® tape, Staples℠, StazOn®, Styrofoam®, SuperTape®, Sure Thing® CD labeling software, Target℠,Terrifically Tacky Tape™, The Vintage Workshop®, Tsukineko®, Woolite®, Velcro®, X-Acto®, Yes!™ paste, Zots™

DEDICATION

In memory of Leah, who taught me that the joy of discovery often comes through patient sifting of the mundane, and my grandfather, Charles Najt, for whom the act of creation was as necessary to life as breathing.

ACKNOWLEDGMENTS

The production of a book is never a solitary pursuit and this book is no exception. First and foremost, I must thank Carolyn Mandarano at The Taunton Press for her enthusiastic response from the very beginning and for the sharp insight and detailed questions that helped me focus and shape an idea into a finished product. I thank Julie Hamilton, my wonderful editor, for her patience, good humor, and incredible attention to detail. I must also thank Jim Childs for being open and taking a chance on an unknown author proposing a topic outside his realm of interest and to the rest of the staff at Taunton for allowing me incredible creative freedom and all the support I needed. Thank you to Chris Thompson, Wendi Mijal, and the rest of the design team at Taunton for their artistic eye and attention to detail and caring for this book as much as I do.

Thank you to Mary Ellen Bartley for agreeing to take on this project and lending her superb eye and photographic skills. The book just wouldn't be the same without her input. Thanks also to two incredibly talented women, Lara Robby and Andrea Chu, for their patient and good-natured assistance with the photo shoots, filling in wherever needed without complaint.

I appreciate the companies that supported my work, generously sending supplies when I shamelessly begged: Paper Source®, Therm O Web, Making Memories®, Chatterbox Inc.®, and Perfect Glue™.

In addition, I am incredibly lucky to have a wonderful web of personal support that stretches from coast to coast, and I am grateful for all of the friends and family who nudged me along and kept me company during long evenings of crafting with deadlines looming. I also appreciate those who lent baby memorabilia; offered insight and opinions; and gave freely of their friendship, support, time, and resources.

Finally, I must thank my husband, Michael, for whom there aren't enough words to articulate his role in my life. I could never have completed this book without his love, encouragement, thoughtful criticism, and willingness to let me turn our home into a craft studio; and I could never imagine a better traveling companion for this journey through life.

CONTENTS

introduction

i meet people all the time who express the desire to make something by hand. Just as quickly as that desire is uttered, the words, "but I'm not very crafty," inevitably follow. The good news is that you don't have to be gifted to create a handmade gift or keepsake. By learning a few basic techniques, using the designs in this book for inspiration, and being patient with yourself you'll be surprised by what you can accomplish. Successful crafting is less about talent and more about practice and a willingness to try something new.

Even though I make my living as a craft designer and stylist, I still crave the gratifying experience of making a gift by hand. It satisfies something very basic—the need to connect with the recipient by carefully creating something meant only for him or her. I'm hardly in the minority, as women (and men) have practiced such hands-on creativity, alone and in groups, over hundreds of years, lovingly crafting special items that are both useful and beautiful gifts.

B Is for Baby came about because of a baby boom in my circle of friends and family. For a long while it was just a list—a list of all the gifts I wished I'd made instead of sending the gift I had purchased. "Wouldn't that be cute," I'd muse, conjuring up a mental image

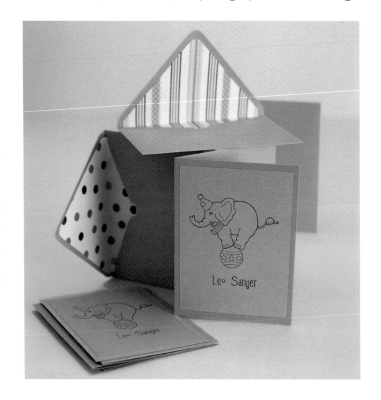

in my head that conflicted with the wrapped gift I was sending. I'd jot it down and think, "next time." Eventually, that list grew very long; and over a serendipitous lunch during a cold winter, the seeds were planted for this book.

Making gifts and creative handmade keepsakes doesn't always have to be difficult or time-consuming. The simplest techniques can yield beautiful and useful items that can't be found in any store. It's my hope that you'll use this book over and over, for all the little ones who come into your life. But I also hope that you'll use the techniques you learn to expand your horizons and enrich your own life. Many of these projects can easily be adapted for personal use, not just for a baby.

Above all, have fun! Gather a couple of friends together, put on a pot of coffee and some music that makes you feel happy, and enjoy being creative. Don't pressure yourself to be perfect. As you become more and more familiar with your tools and materials you'll be delighted with the way your imagination takes flight and the lovely things that will come from your own two hands.

GETTING STARTED

P reparation is essential for a fun and enjoyable crafting experience. It's frustrating to begin a project, only to find that you don't have what you need to finish it. More often than not, the half-completed project joins all the others, waiting for the rainy day that never comes.

To avoid that common trap, first gather all of the tools and materials you'll need to do the project from start to finish. Most of the projects in this book are made from materials easily found at your local craft store. Others can be purchased online. If you're not sure where to purchase a certain item, Resources on p. 171 will help you find everything you need. If you're an experienced crafter, some materials, such as adhesives, may be interchangeable. If you're a beginner, each project lists the materials that are easiest to work with for that particular project. As you become more proficient, use what feels most comfortable for you.

tools

THE ESSENTIALS

BONE FOLDER

This inexpensive tool is a must if you're working with paper. It allows you to create precise folds and creases. It's also useful for burnishing, smoothing out edges, and defining corners when making journals or books.

CORK-BACKED METAL RULER

If you're working with paper or fabric, a cork-backed metal ruler is a good investment. The cork prevents slippage, allowing precise cuts with both straight craft blades and rotary cutters.

CUTTING BLADES

Some people love working with small craft blades. Personally, I prefer large utility blades with straight edges to cut heavy cardstock and boards. Rotary cutters are great for paper and fabric. For the best value, buy rotary cutters that allow you to switch from a straight blade to a decorative one.

CUTTING MAT

A self-healing cutting mat not only protects your surface area but usually comes with markings that help you align fabric or paper to ensure an even cut. A small mat is generally fine for many of the paper projects and small-scale fabric projects in this book. Some mats also fold up for easy storage.

SCISSORS

Scissors are my favorite tool. I own 16 pairs, not counting a collection of paper edgers. The average crafter, however, needs only cutting shears and embroidery scissors for fabric projects and one large and one fine-tipped pair of scissors for paper projects. However, if your budget allows, purchase pinking shears and scalloped-edge scissors too. They're great for giving a decorative edge to fabric, ribbon, and paper.

HOLE PUNCHES

There are lots of decorative punches on the market, but the three I use most frequently are the $1/16$ in. round, $1/8$ in. round, and $1/4$ in. round. They're great for all sorts of paper projects as well as for creating designs in felt.

PAINTBRUSHES

I use inexpensive, bristle paintbrushes for everything from painting to gluing to decoupaging. Unless you're undertaking a fine art project, purchase cheap brushes from the craft store. (Look for the variety packs. They're economical and include most of what you'll need.) In general, you'll want to have flat brushes in various widths as well as a few fine-tipped brushes for detail work and touch-ups. Disposable foam brushes are useful, too, for general painting and decoupaging.

SANDPAPER

Sandpaper comes in a variety of grits with corresponding numbers. The higher the grit number, the smoother the sandpaper. Generally, fine to super-fine grade sandpaper (150 to 600 grit) is all you'll need for crafting. You'll use it to lightly distress paper and to prepare surfaces for paint or decoupage. Foam emery boards (found in beauty supply stores and drugstores) are also useful for distressing the edges of paper or other delicate items.

IRON

Don't start a sewing or fabric project without a basic iron; you'll need it to help you smooth out the kinks.

USEFUL ADDITIONS

SEWING MACHINE

Even inexpensive sewing machines will meet a crafter's basic needs. And a machine is useful for more than fabric; you can sew on paper, cards, and crepe paper, expanding your crafting options.

DECORATIVE BLADES FOR ROTARY CUTTER

Rotary cutters are great, general-purpose tools, and you can get even more for your money with the various interchangeable decorative blades that can be used on either paper or fabric. Scalloped, pinking, deckle, perforating, and scoring are just a few of the blades available.

DISAPPEARING-INK PENS

These are great for tracing around stencils, drawing guidelines and lettering, and any time in which you don't want ink to show on the final project. These pens can be used on fabric and some brands can be used on paper and other craft surfaces. Depending on the brand, the lines usually disappear between 24 hours and 72 hours after application.

PAPER SEWING KIT

Complete with a needle tool for making holes in paper and a ruler with prespaced holes, a paper sewing kit is helpful when adding details such as thread or ribbons to paper projects.

ALPHABET RUBBER STAMPS

Available in a wide variety of fonts and sizes, alphabet stamps can be used to personalize projects. They work on paper, fabric, and even unusual surfaces like wood, rubber, and metal when the correct ink pads are used.

CRAFT PUNCHES

Punches are useful for punching out various shapes (especially circles!) and designs in all different sizes, from very small to very large. You can use craft punches for paper projects and decoupage.

STENCIL FILM OR ACETATE

When crafting in bulk, such as creating announcements, sturdy templates are needed to withstand extensive use. Packaged stencil film is available in craft stores, but you can also recycle acetate lids from gift boxes or other packaging instead.

MINI QUILTING IRON

With a tiny flat head and a long handle, a mini iron gets into spaces a regular iron can't and works well for detail work, such as appliqué.

TRANSFER PAPER

Transfer paper is useful for transferring designs to wood and fabric. Convenient and easy to use, this paper allows amateurs to obtain professional results when painting, stitching, or placing designs. Some transfer paper works with a special pen (and transfer marks are covered by paint or stitching); others leave erasable markings that can be helpful when trying to work out design placement.

Usually found in craft stores in the paint department, fine-tip applicators are useful when precision is required, either with paint or glue.

materials

PAPER

Paper is one of my favorite mediums to work with. There's a staggering variety to choose from, and I routinely add to my collection, whether I have a specific use in mind or not. Ranging from inexpensive scrapbook paper to precious fine art papers that demand a special use, they're all great to work with! For archival results, choose acid-free papers.

SCRAPBOOK PAPER AND CARDSTOCK

Even if you don't do much scrap-booking, that shouldn't stop you from regularly using scrapbook papers and cardstock in projects of all sorts. It's extremely versatile and can be used for cards and announcements, gift tags, labels and packaging, and decoupage. It's inexpensive and there's a style for everyone. It usually comes in 8½-in. by 11-in. and 12-in. by 12-in. sheets; most of them are acid free.

VELLUM

Most stores that sell scrapbook paper sell vellum. It's a semitranslucent paper you can print on, stamp, or use as an overlay to soften the colors and designs of paper underneath it. It comes in a variety of sizes, colors, patterns, and weights.

WALLPAPER

Wallpaper isn't just for walls; use remnants to cover boxes, for decoupage, to make lampshades or book covers, or to cover tabletops or tray bottoms. The possibilities are endless. Look for remnants at flea markets or online sources, such as eBay®. You can also check with local paint and wallpaper stores; many of them discard old sample books and will give them to you for free.

ART PAPER

Generally sold in large sheets and in a variety of textures, patterns, weights, and colors, these papers range from inexpensive to ultra-pricey. Some are machine-made, whereas others are hand-made or painted by hand. Because of the wide variety available, ask a salesperson if the paper is a good choice for your specific project.

GIFT WRAP

A number of companies are producing large gift wrap sheets with a matte finish and a heavier weight than traditional gift wrap. You can use them to make cards and cover books, to decoupage with, to laminate, and to make labels and packaging.

KRAFT PAPER

Kraft paper is indispensable for protecting work surfaces and making templates and it's a must for your craft bin. Usually sold in rolls, it can be found in craft supply stores or wherever office or postal supplies are sold (sometimes it goes by the alias "shipping paper" because packages are often wrapped in it before being mailed).

Helpful Hints

ASK QUESTIONS WHEN SHOPPING.
New products come on the market all the time and there may be something that will save you time or money or help you achieve more professional results. Don't hesitate to ask salespeople or experts for advice.

GET TO KNOW YOUR TOOLS.
Tools are only helpful if you know how to use them. Practice on scrap materials before embarking on the final project.

BUY EXTRA MATERIALS.
When budget allows, buy extra materials for a project in case something has to be redone or inspiration strikes.

PRACTICE DESIGNS BEFOREHAND.
Using scrap materials, work out the project designs and placement of elements before undertaking the final project.

HAVE CONFIDENCE IN YOURSELF.
The best gifts are those that come from the heart. Use the designs presented here as a starting point, but don't be afraid to add your own creative spark or style. Most of the projects in this book can easily take on a new style with a simple change of paper, fabric, or color palette, allowing plenty of room for self-expression.

FABRIC

You can never have too much fabric! You will find a number of projects in this book that incorporate fabric. I generally use inexpensive cotton print fabric, not only because it saves money but because of the great variety of designs available. Many crafting projects require only small bits of fabric, so be on the lookout for "fat quarters" (quilting fabric cut to 18 in. by 22 in., or 1/2 yd. cut in half) in the quilting section of craft and fabric stores. It's also worth hanging on to small remnants; they can be used in decoupage projects or used for appliqué.

FELT

Felt is another incredibly versatile material for crafting. However, wool felt is the best. It costs more than standard craft felt, but it is unparalleled in terms of durability, texture, and ease of handling. It's worth the investment if you're planning to make something meant to last.

RIBBON

Nothing completes a project better than the perfect ribbon embellishment. Ribbon comes in a wide variety of textures, colors, and patterns. Grosgrain, cotton, rayon, velvet, and satin ribbons are all easy to glue on but respond best when used with a quick-setting fabric glue meant for delicate items (such as Fabri-Tac™). If in doubt about what kind of adhesive to use on a particular ribbon (and some will be better sewn on than glued on), experiment with a small piece before using it on the final project.

PAINT

Unless you're painting large projects (such as furniture) or have access to sample sizes of latex paint, inexpensive acrylic craft paints are a good choice. Available in an extensive color palette, paints can be blended to create custom colors. Most brands also carry textile mediums that can be mixed into the paints, making them suitable for fabrics as well.

ADHESIVES

Many adhesives have overlapping abilities; and eventually, you'll develop favorites. However, it's always a good idea to choose acid-free adhesives for projects meant to last. The following are some of my favorite adhesives and what I use them for.

HEATNBOND® ULTRA-HOLD IRON-ON ADHESIVE

This heat activated adhesive with a paper backing allows a no-sew bond for fabric and felt that's durable and washable. It's incredibly effective and easy to use. Non-paper-backed rolls of tape are available for no-sew hemming as well.

PEELnSTICK™ DOUBLE-SIDED ADHESIVE SHEETS

These all-purpose adhesive sheets create an immediate, lasting bond. I love their ease and durability and I use them with paper as well as fabric. Since they're paper backed, it's easy to draw designs directly onto the sheets and then cut them out.

ACID-FREE DOUBLE-SIDED ADHESIVE TAPE

This incredibly strong tape comes in widths ranging from $\frac{1}{8}$ in. to 1 in. I use it when I want a super-strong hold with no mess. It can be used to secure paper, fabric, glitter, beads, and ribbon. Look for brands such as SuperTape®, Terrifically Tacky Tape™, and Incredi-Tape.

YES!™PASTE

Yes! paste is a nontoxic, acid-free paste that's permanently flexible, won't curl papers, and won't yellow with age. It's thicker than liquid glue so it doesn't run but it can be thinned with warm water. It needs to be applied with a paste brush and can be used with leather, wood, metal, glass, paper, and fabric.

MOD PODGE®

The gold standard in decoupage, Mod Podge comes in a variety of finishes from matte to sparkle. There are special formulations for paper as well as a formula for decoupaging with fabric.

PERFECT GLUE™

Available in three formulas, Perfect Glue can easily replace a hot glue gun. And although it can be used on virtually any surface (including paper and fabric), I use it most for tough-to-glue surfaces and embellishments, such as metal, Styrofoam®, leather, ceramic, wood, and rubber.

ZOTS™ AND GLUE DOTS®

These easy-to-use, flexible adhesive dots are great for paper and other craft projects. They come in several varieties and sizes; some are suitable for delicate items such as paper and photographs, whereas others can handle heavier crafting tasks, such as securing embellishments.

FABRI-TAC™

A permanent, quick-drying, washable glue that's excellent for gluing delicate fabrics and trimmings, Fabic-Tac doesn't stain or soak into fabrics. However, it has a tendency to string when dispensing, but a dab of petroleum jelly on the top of the dispensing tip helps prevent this.

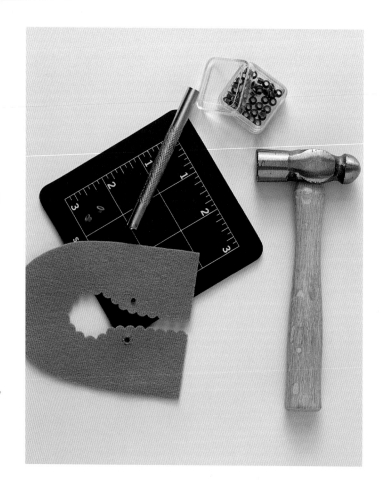

crafting with computers

I've started using a computer in many of my crafting projects over the last few years. Professionally, I couldn't live without it or my scanner and color printer. There are so many fun fonts available as well as desktop publishing software that's easy even for beginners.

If I had to choose only one computer accessory that I couldn't live without, I would choose a color inkjet printer. I have a user-friendly consumer model that was inexpensive, but it's a true workhorse. These printers can be used to create iron-on transfers, magnets, labels, cards, and announcements.

You can also print your own photos or print on fabric sheets and ribbons. Having a color printer will immediately enhance your options in a number of crafts. And if your computer skills are limited to surfing the Internet or typing up documents, invest in a simple how-to book to increase your confidence and skill level. You'll be surprised by how much you can design with a simple word-processing program.

COMPUTER TUTOR

Economizing on paper means knowing how to create multiple sets of text on each sheet. The easiest way to compose and center text is to insert "text boxes" on your document. These boxes act as independent work spaces and can be sized to the exact dimension of your announcement or card. You can create as many as will fit on a single sheet of paper.

Want to center your text within each text box? Click anywhere inside the text box and choose the centering tool from your toolbar. Type out the information in each text box. Afterwards, but before printing, format the text box to remove lines bordering each box. Then print and cut out your individual text boxes according to the instructions.

tips & techniques

MAKING MASTER TEMPLATES

Before beginning a project with a template, you'll need to enlarge the appropriate template(s), as directed on the template outline, using a copier or scanner. If you'll be making a master template out of heavy cardstock or cardboard, you will first need to cut out the enlarged template, trace it onto cardstock or cardboard, and then cut it out again along the trace lines. If you're making a master template on stencil film or acetate, simply trace over the enlarged template and cut it out as directed.

TEMPLATES WITH TEXT

Most templates should be cut along the exterior lines. However, when making cardboard or cardstock templates for announcements or projects for which text or image placement is a key part of the design, cutting out the *interior* of the template will allow you to place it over text and images so you can center them and see what the final project will look like. If, however, you're using clear stencil film, go ahead and cut around the exterior lines because you'll be able to see your text through the film.

CUTTING WITH SCISSORS

Many people are intimidated by cutting things out with scissors. Practice will increase your confidence, but a quick way to get smoother results, especially with curved objects, is to move the material you're cutting, not your hand.

USING A BONE FOLDER

When using a bone folder to score paper, place your ruler along the intended fold line and run the tip of your bone folder along the ruler's edge. Your paper will show a slight indentation; this is your fold line. As a burnishing tool, use the tip to smooth out edges and corners. You can also run the edge or flat sides over areas that are glued, smoothing out any air bubbles.

DETERMINING PAPER GRAIN

Machine-made papers generally have a grain, a built-in directional structure. The grain makes it easier to fold or tear paper in one direction than in the other. Folding paper along the grain makes the cleanest creases. (If you need to fold paper in both directions, use your bone folder to score it before folding.) To determine grain, bring two of the paper's parallel edges together (without folding), such as top to bottom, and gently apply pressure. Release and repeat with parallel edges on the other sides. Your paper will exhibit more resistance to being bent in one direction than the other. The grain runs parallel to the direction that offers the least resistance. This is especially important to know in bookbinding, as paper and boards need to be glued with their grains running parallel; otherwise, the finished product will never lie flat.

PREPARING FABRICS

When making washable fabric projects, you will first want to wash the fabrics to remove sizing and allow the fabric to shrink before sewing. If the item you are making is meant to be worn by Baby or will rest near Baby's skin, consider washing the fabric with a delicate detergent such as Woolite®.

PAINTING

If you'll be painting furniture or objects before adding embellishments, I highly recommend that you prime the piece first with one or two coats of latex primer. Priming increases the durability of your piece as well as prepares it to accept paint. It also aids in a streak-free, even finish.

CHOOSING A COLOR PALETTE

The color scheme you choose for your project can completely alter its look and feel. Nontraditional shades of traditional colors and unusual color pairings can instantly elevate the look of basic projects and create a more contemporary feel. So don't be afraid to take some chances with your color palette.

Need inspiration? Look around and see what you respond to—in advertisements, magazine articles, scrapbook papers, your home decor, clothing, nature, and so on. Once you consciously pay attention to color, you'll start to notice unusual and arresting combinations.

techniques in action

The techniques pictured here will help clarify directions that might seem confusing or are new to you. Although specific projects are shown, some of the techniques, such as "notching fabric," are used in numerous projects throughout the book.

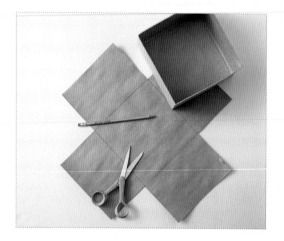

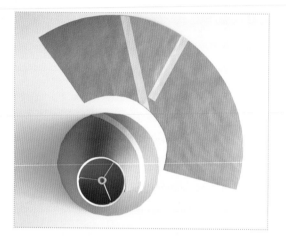

Box Templates

Place the box base or lid in the center of a piece of kraft paper and trace around it with a pencil. With a ruler, extend the lines from the corners of the outline to the height of the box (or the height of the box lid if you are making a template for the lid), and add a $1/2$-in. overhang on all sides. Cut out the areas between the line intersections.

Lampshade Templates

Place the straight edge of a piece of kraft paper along the back seam of the lampshade and secure it to the lampshade with tape. Wrap the paper around the lampshade, holding it in place with more tape. If necessary, cut additional pieces of paper to fill in any gaps and tape them to the kraft paper base. Trim the paper along the top and bottom edges of the lampshade, then remove the kraft paper base and any added pieces from the shade as a unit. Make sure the paper template is taped securely together.

MAKING SHOES

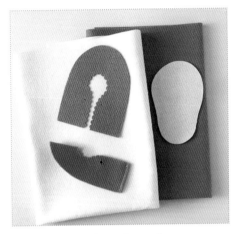

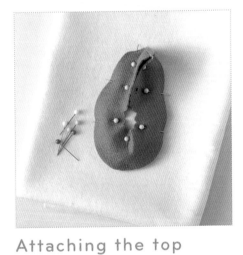

Sewing the heel

Fold the shoe cutout inside out and stitch a $1/8$-in. seam along the back edge.

Attaching the top to the sole

With the shoe cutout still inside out, attach the top of the shoe to the sole using straight pins, then sew around the perimeter of the shoe with a $1/4$-in. seam allowance.

Assembling the boy booties

For these shoes, all the elements are assembled before any sewing takes place. Once each cutout looks like the shoe pictured above, sewing commences—the shoe cutout is folded inside out and the heel is sewn as pictured in the left photo above. The soles are attached to these shoes in the same manner as shown in the center photo above.

MAKING A JOURNAL

Making accordian folds

Line up your ruler vertically 4³/4 in. from the short edge and use the bone folder to score a folding line on the paper, following the ruler's edge. Fold the paper to the right along the scored line. Continue scoring lines with the bone folder along each folded edge and fold the paper back and forth until you've reached the end of the paper strip.

Trimming corners on a diagonal

Center one of the book-board panels on the paper and trace around the board with a pencil. Remove the board and trim the paper corners on a diagonal, leaving enough paper to cover the corners of the board.

Using a bone folder on corners

Once the paper has been glued to the front of the board and the long sides of the paper have been adhered, use the tip of the bone folder to fold in all the corners of the paper surrounding the book-board piece (creating clean, tight corners when the paper is folded.) Apply more paste to the short edges and fold them over the book-board panel, smoothing them with the bone folder if necessary.

MAKING YOUR NAME

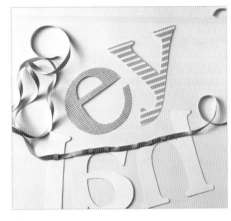

Padding the letters

Lay each papier-mâché letter facedown on top of the batting and trace around each letter with the disappearing ink pen. Cut the letters out on the trace lines. Glue the batting cutouts to the surface of each papier-mâché letter using fabric glue. Trim any excess batting from the edges if necessary.

Notching fabric

When a project refers to notching fabric or paper, it means you should cut slits in the fabric or paper as shown. This allows you to curve around edges or corners without bunching and gives a much cleaner look.

Making loops for hanging

Make loops of ribbon just wide enough for the ribbon to pass through. Glue the ends of the ribbon together to form the loop. (Some letters, such as *i* and *l* will only need one loop; others, such as *m* and *w* will need two loops for balance when hung.) Glue the loops to the back of each letter, aligning each set of loops so the ribbon will be consistent when hung.

Is for Announcements

Nine long months go by, and when Baby arrives, you're ready to shout it from the rooftops! Use one of these announcements to spread your good news in style. There are options for everyone, whether you like to plan ahead or wait till the last minute.

announcing the arri...
of our daught...

TOOLS & MATERIALS

- ✓ Computer and printer (optional)
- ✓ Heavy cardstock, 8½-in. by 11-in. sheets, in the color of your choice (one sheet yields four announcements)
- ✓ Diaper Announcement and Card for Diaper Announcement templates (p. 158)
- ✓ Heavy cardstock or stencil film, 8½-in. by 11-in. sheet, for master template
- ✓ Patterned cardstock or paper, 8½-in. by 11-in. sheets (one sheet for each announcement)
- ✓ Pencil
- ✓ Ruler
- ✓ Rotary blade or scissors
- ✓ Cutting mat
- ✓ Bone folder
- ✓ ¼-in. double-sided tape or other adhesive
- ✓ ⅛-in. hole punch
- ✓ Diaper pin or ribbon for embellishment
- ✓ A6 envelopes (4¾ in. by 6½ in.) for mailing

DIAPER CARD

 ll thumbs? Get a head start on diaper changes by practicing with these whimsical precursors of what lies ahead. Cheerful patterns and colors sweeten the task.

1. If you are using a computer to compose birth information, see "Computer Tutor," on p. 15, for guidelines on how to arrange multiple sets of text on a single page. Type and print out four sets of the birth information on the sheet of heavy cardstock; then cut the sheet into cards measuring 3 in. by 4½ in., with the text centered in each card. If you are writing the birth information by hand, cut the cards first, then write the text.

2. Enlarge the Diaper Announcement template as directed, copy it onto heavy cardstock or stencil film, and cut it out along the trace lines; this is your master template (see "Making Master Templates," on p. 16 for tips). Place the template on the wrong

Make Ahead

All diapers can be made ahead. After Baby's arrival, print out the birth information onto the cardstock and make the announcement cards as directed.

side of the patterned paper and lightly trace around it with a pencil. Cut it out along the trace lines, using either a ruler and rotary blade or with scissors.

3. Fold the original Diaper Announcement template along the dotted lines and place it on top of the patterned cutout (be sure the wrong side of your patterned cut-out diaper is facing up). Using the folded template as a guide, use the bone folder to score the patterned cutout along the edges where the folds will be. Fold in the ends and use double-sided tape or other adhesive to secure the diaper ends together.

4. Punch holes in the announcement information card as shown on the Card for Diaper Announcement template. Insert a diaper pin in the holes or thread ribbon through the holes and tie it in a bow. (If you are using a diaper pin, it's a good idea to make sure your pin is long enough to span the holes shown in the template. If not, you'll need to adjust the holes to suit the length of your pin.)

5. Slip the card inside the diaper with the pin or bow resting on the top edge of the diaper.

Just Your Style

If you'd like to add an extra decorative touch, trim the sides of the diaper with scallop-edged scissors before folding.

TOOLS & MATERIALS

✓ Patterned paper, 2¼ in. by 4½ in. (one piece for each announcement)

✓ Ruler

✓ Rotary blade

✓ Cutting mat

✓ Plain matchbox, measuring 2¼ in. by 1¼ in.

✓ ¼-in. double-sided tape

✓ Solid colored paper, 2¼ in. by ½ in. (one piece for each announcement)

✓ Decorative edged scissors (optional)

✓ Craft glue (optional)

✓ Small buttons or other embellishments

✓ Complementary cardstock for interior of matchbox, 2⅛ in. by 1⅛ in. (one piece for each announcement)

✓ Computer and printer

✓ Diaper pin (no longer than 2⅛ in.)

✓ Small padded envelope for mailing

MATCHBOX ANNOUNCEMENT

 good things come in small packages as evidenced by this unusual birth announcement. Mail in a padded white or pastel envelope to announce this special delivery.

1. Cut a piece of patterned paper to 2¼ in. wide by 4½ in. long. Adhere one of the short edges of the paper to the bottom of the matchbox cover with double-sided tape. Be sure to align the edges of the paper with the top and bottom edges of the matchbox cover. Wrap the paper around the matchbox cover, overlap the ends, and secure them with more double-sided tape.

2. To embellish, cut a piece of solid colored paper into a strip ½ in. wide by 4½ in. long. Trim one long edge of the paper strip with decorative scissors, if desired, and layer it over the base paper on the bottom of the matchbox cover. Use craft glue, to adhere small buttons or other embellishments, if desired, as shown in the photo on the facing page.

Make Ahead

All matchboxes can be covered and embellished before Baby's arrival. Complete the boxes with the small announcement cards after Baby is born, and wait to buy the diaper pins if you want them to be gender specific.

Lee & Jamie Webb
welcomed the arrival of
Jason Baxter
on April 17, 2006
7 lbs, 15 oz of pure joy!

3. To create the announcement card for the interior of the matchbox, use a small font size (approximately 10 points) to print Baby's birth information onto the cardstock. See "Computer Tutor," on p. 15, for guidelines on arranging multiple copies of text on one sheet. Repeat the information approximately 12 times on each 8½-in. by 11-in. sheet of paper. Cut the sheet into cards, each measuring 2⅛ in. long by 1⅛ in. wide, with the text centered in each card. Secure the card to the bottom of the matchbox with a small strip of double-sided tape. Enclose a diaper pin in the matchbox as a finishing touch.

- Heavy cardstock, 8½-in. by 11-in. sheets (one sheet for each announcement)
- Ruler
- Rotary cutter
- Cutting mat
- Therm O Web PeelnStick double-sided adhesive sheets, 5½-in. by 8¾-in. sheet (one sheet yields two announcements)
- Decorative fabric, 4 in. by 5½ in. (one piece for each announcement)
- Close-up baby photos
- Craft glue or double-sided tape
- Heavy vellum, 8½-in. by 11-in. sheets (one sheet yields 15 to 20 announcements)
- Computer and printer
- Buttons or other embellishments
- A7 envelope for mailing (for 5-in. by 7-in. announcements)

PHOTO ANNOUNCEMENT

 amily and friends will clamor for a glimpse of your newborn. Send them a photograph with this simple announcement made from paper and fabric. Pick a favorite cotton or linen print and let it guide your color palette.

1. Trim the cardstock to 5 in. by 7 in., or desired announcement size.

2. Remove the paper backing from one side of the double-sided adhesive sheet and adhere it to a piece of decorative fabric, covering the fabric completely and smoothing out any wrinkles or air bubbles with your fingers. Use a ruler and a rotary cutter to cut the fabric into two pieces, each measuring 4 in. by 5½ in. Remove the backing from the other side of the adhesive and adhere the fabric to the cardstock (double-sided adhesive will keep your fabric from fraying), with the fabric placed ¼ in. from the top edge of the cardstock, allowing room for the birth information at the bottom.

3. Trim the photo to 3 in. by 4¼ in. and adhere it to the fabric with craft glue or double-sided tape.

4. Type out the birth information and print it onto a sheet of vellum, repeating until the page is filled, allowing about ¾ in. of space

between each line of text. Use the rotary cutter and ruler to cut the text into ½-in. by 8½-in. strips.

5. Attach a vellum strip containing the birth information to the bottom front of the card, folding the ends over the back about ¼ in. (trimming, if necessary). Secure the strip to the back of the card with double-sided tape or craft glue. Glue small embellishments, such as buttons, on top of the vellum strip to anchor it to the front of the card.

TOOLS & MATERIALS

- Master footprint made with colored ink
- Computer scanner
- Computer and color printer
- Ivory or white cardstock, 8½-in. by 11-in. sheets (one sheet yields four announcements)
- Ruler
- Rotary cutter
- Cutting mat
- Patterned cardstock, 12-in. by 12-in. sheets (one sheet yields four announcements)
- Solid colored cardstock, 12-in. by 12-in. sheets (one sheet yields two announcements)
- ¼-in. double-sided tape or clear adhesive dots (such as Glue Dots)
- Decorative ribbon
- A6 envelopes for mailing

FOOTPRINT ANNOUNCEMENT

sing a baby's footprint for an announcement isn't a new concept, but it's usually seen in black. For an updated version of a classic, use colored ink that reflects your personal aesthetic. The celery green shown above yields a soft, yet contemporary look for either a boy or girl.

1. Create a master footprint of Baby using white paper and the colored ink of your choice (if you plan ahead and bring these items to the hospital, one of the staff there may do it for you). Scan the master footprint and save it to your computer as a jpg file. If you don't have a scanner at home, ask your local copy shop to create one and put it on a disc for you.

2. On your computer, insert four text boxes in a document, each measuring 3 in. wide by 5 in. long (see "Computer Tutor," on p. 15). Use the centering tool and type in Baby's birth announcement information near the bottom of each text box, using your desired font, color, and size. Insert the scanned footprint image above the birth information. Format the text boxes to remove border lines, then print them out onto ivory or white cardstock. Trim the cardstock to create four cards, each measuring 3 in. wide by 5 in. long.

3. Trim the patterned cardstock to measure $4\frac{1}{4}$ in. by 6 in. and the colored cardstock to measure $4\frac{1}{2}$ in. by $6\frac{1}{4}$ in. Center and mount the patterned cardstock onto the solid colored cardstock using double-sided tape or Glue Dots.

4. Layer the birth information card over the cardstock, not quite centered, with slightly more space at the bottom of the card than at the top. Attach the top center edge of the birth information card to the cardstock layers with a small piece of double-sided tape or an adhesive dot. Use another adhesive dot or a bit of double-sided tape to secure a bow or knot at the top of the card

Getting the Footprint

Getting a clean footprint from a wriggling baby isn't the easiest thing to do. For the best result, get the footprint while your baby is sleeping. If you do it while the baby is awake, it helps to have one person holding his or her foot steady while the other makes the footprint. If Baby is crying during your attempt, remind yourself that it is a momentary situation and worth the wailing. Your baby's foot will never be so small again!

Is for Baby Book

It doesn't take much to turn an ordinary photo album into a one-of-a-kind, personal memento. Simple touches make all the difference; and if you're giving the album as a gift, a few premade pages will give a busy mom a head start.

TOOLS & MATERIALS

- ✓ Photo of Baby, 2 in. by 3 in.
- ✓ Solid cardstock, 3-in. by 4-in. pieces, two pieces in complementary colors
- ✓ Mini scallop scissors
- ✓ Acid-free all-purpose adhesive
- ✓ Ruler
- ✓ Rotary cutter or craft knife
- ✓ Cutting mat
- ✓ Plain photo album (of any material)
- ✓ Acid-free label for name
- ✓ Fine-tipped pen
- ✓ Decorative ribbon, equal to the length of the album, plus 6 in.
- ✓ Fabric scissors
- ✓ Fabri-Tac or other fabric glue
- ✓ Decorative patterned paper, larger than the album pages, 2 sheets (optional)
- ✓ Yes! paste (optional)
- ✓ Paste brush (optional)

1. Glue Baby's photo onto a piece of solid cardstock. Use the mini scallop scissors to trim the edges of the cardstock just around the photo, then glue that layer onto the other piece of solid cardstock. Using the rotary cutter or craft knife on the cutting mat, trim around the edges, $1/8$ in. to $1/4$ in. from the scalloped edge. Glue the layered photo onto the front of the photo album, centering it in the upper third of the album.

2. Hand-write Baby's name on the label of your choice with the fine-tipped pen and glue it just underneath the layered photo.

3. Cut a length of ribbon 1 in. longer than the length of the album and center it along the bound album edge. Wrap the ends around the inside of the front cover and use fabric glue to adhere the ends to the interior (you'll cover the ribbon ends with decorative paper later).

4. Cut a 6-in. length of ribbon and tie it into a knot. Trim the ends, as desired, and glue the knot over the ribbon on the front cover, adhering it with fabric glue.

5. If you wish to create decorative end papers, open the album and measure the height of the interior pages and the length from the left edge of the front cover to the right edge of the first page. Cut two pieces of decorative paper to those measurements and fold them in half so the short edges meet. Use Yes! paste to glue one piece to the inside of the front cover (over the ribbon ends), extending it over the first page and glue the second piece to the interior of the back cover, extending it over the last page.

Give Mom a Head Start

Blank pages in book and album gifts are intimidating for most people and are often the perfect excuse to procrastinate filling them up. Give Mom a head start by creating a few premade pages that she can mount in her book (using acid-free adhesive or double-sided tape). Not only will you help her get started but you'll also inspire her by showing her what she can create.

Keep it simple

The pages shown below don't require a great deal of effort. A miniature cardstock hanger cutout holds baby's first tee, which can be secured to patterned paper with glue dots or a bit of fabric glue.

New babies and new moms get lots of cards

Help mom keep her favorites in one place with a pocket page that keeps them together without requiring that each one be glued in the book. For this option, simply cut a pocket to the desired size from a piece of

patterned paper or fabric and glue only the sides and bottom to a sheet of solid paper. Embellish as desired. You can also create layouts for standard-size photos by layering patterned paper "frames" over a base paper. Mom can then just glue photos over the patterned paper cutouts. You can also type out a list of "firsts" with blank lines next to them on a piece of solid paper and glue it onto patterned paper. Mom can fill them out as new events take place.

Just Your Style

There are plenty of other ways to personalize an album cover if a photograph isn't quite your style. Here are a few suggestions:

- Monogrammed charms or lockets (apply with a strong adhesive such as Perfect Glue).

- Unusual buttons (try a row of three, placed either vertically or horizontally).

- Decorative cutouts made from fabric or paper.

- A monogram from a vintage handkerchief framed with ribbon or a small metal frame.

- Acid-free cardstock with Baby's name written in calligraphy.

Is for
Customized Disc

There are plenty of CDs on the market for children, but none will touch a mother's heart more than a selection of music chosen by you. Custom CDs are also perfect for sharing your heart song with family and friends as a birth announcement. Specially designed packaging goes beyond the merely useful and adds an extra personal touch.

Jacob's First Music

Be Mine
Beautiful Life
Blue Pony
The Kid
So Are You to Me
Somewhere Over the Rainbow
What a Wonderful World
Isn't She Lovely
Godmamed
Rocking
Blackbird

Max's First Music

It is in learning music
that many youthful hearts
learn to love.

TOOLS & MATERIALS

- ✓ Computer with CD burner and Internet service
- ✓ Blank CD
- ✓ CD label software
- ✓ Self-adhesive CD labels
- ✓ Color printer
- ✓ Patterned cardstock, two 12-in. by 12-in. sheets
- ✓ Ruler
- ✓ Rotary cutter
- ✓ Cutting mat
- ✓ 1/8-in. double-sided tape
- ✓ Bone folder
- ✓ CD Package template (p. 159)
- ✓ Eyelets, 1/8 in. or 3/16 in., in complementary color (optional)
- ✓ Eyelet setter and setting mat (optional)
- ✓ Small hammer for setting eyelets (optional)
- ✓ Thin decorative ribbon
- ✓ 1/8-in. hole punch (optional)
- ✓ Complementary solid cardstock, 8½-in. by 11-in. sheet
- ✓ Decorative-edge scissors (optional)

1. Select music from a downloadable music service such as iTunes® and burn the selections onto a blank disc.

2. Make a CD label, following the directions on your label software, and print it out. (Consider adding the recipient's name to the label, titling your CD, or displaying a photo of Baby.)

3. For the packaging, cut one of the sheets of patterned cardstock into two strips, each measuring 5½ in. by 12-in. (Set the leftover 1-in. strip aside for later use.) With the wrong sides of the strips facing, tape the two pieces of the cardstock together with double-sided tape. This will create a strip that has a pattern on both sides.

   Note: This is an optional step. It will make for a sturdier CD holder, but it isn't essential. If you prefer, simply cut one strip of patterned cardstock and proceed to the next step.

4. Using the ruler and the bone folder, score a line on the wrong side of the cardstock strip 5¼ in. from the left edge and fold the cardstock from left to right. Use the bone folder to score a line where the folded edge ends. Fold the right edge to the left to create the package flap. If desired, use the leftover

1-in. strip from Step 3 to add visual interest to your CD package by wrapping the strip around the front of the CD holder horizontally and using double-sided tape to adhere it.

5. Create the pocket for the CD using the second piece of patterned cardstock. Cut it into a strip measuring 4 in. by 5½ in. Use the ruler and bone folder to score lines on the sides and bottom edge of the strip, ¼ in. from the edge. Trim the bottom corners along the fold lines (see the CD Package template for guidance). Turn the scored edges in toward the wrong side and apply ⅛-in. double-sided tape on those edges; tape the pocket to the interior of the CD holder.

6. Using the CD Package template as a guide, add the eyelets to the front of your CD holder following the manufacturer's directions for your eyelet setter. (You can also refer to "Trade Secret," on p. 55, for instructions on setting eyelets.) String ribbon through the eyelet holes and either glue or tape the ribbon to the inside of the package. If you choose not to use eyelets, punch holes with a ⅛-in. hole punch and string the ribbon through.

7. Type up a song list on your computer and print it out on the complementary solid cardstock. Trim the edges, using decorative-edge scissors, if desired, and tape the list to the inside of the CD holder, covering the ribbon and eyelet on the left side.

8. Place the finished CD in the pocket and tie the ribbon ends into a bow to close the CD holder.

Not Just for Music

Looking for a creative way to send or keep photos of your little one? Follow the music CD packaging directions, but instead of burning music onto your disc, save copies of photos on the disc.

If desired, choose one of your favorite photos and print it out onto the CD label, following the directions that come with your label software. Finish with an interior label (replacing the song list) that lists your baby's birth information, a personal note, or a line from a nursery rhyme.

Is for Decoupage

Decoupage is the simple art of gluing paper cutouts to an object, but the results are anything but plain. It's an easily learned skill and the possibilities are endless. From letter cutouts to baby photo collages, let your imagination run wild with what you can cut out and where to glue it.

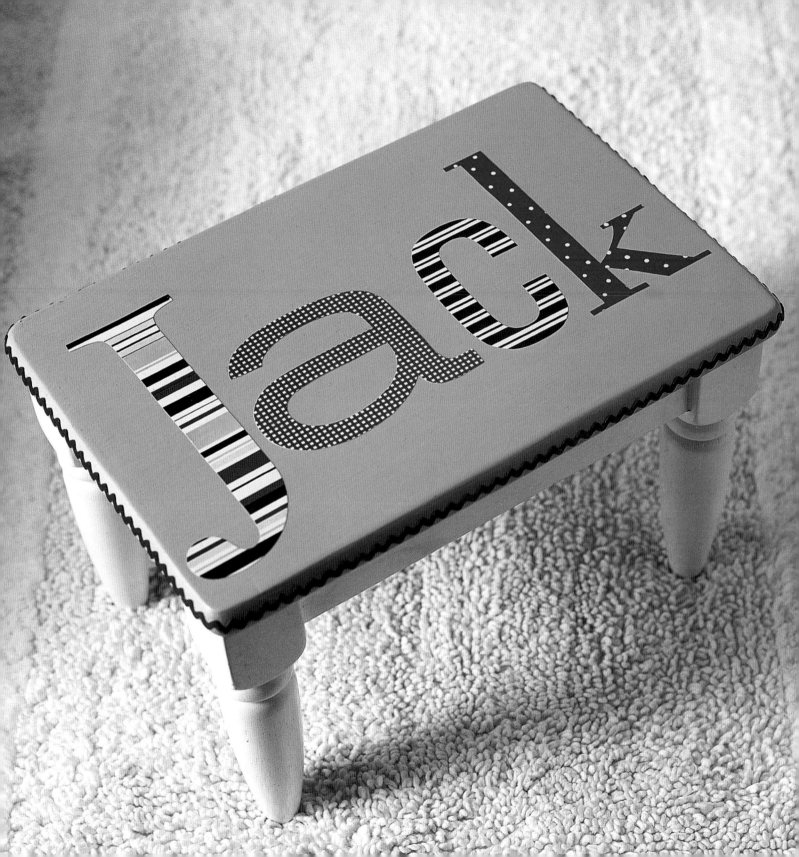

✓ Wooden step stool

✓ Fine-grade sanding block

✓ Latex primer

✓ Painters' tape

✓ Latex paint in two colors

✓ Template for each letter in name (use a computer or create freehand)

✓ Cardstock, 8 ½-in. by 11-in. sheets (one sheet for each letter in name)

✓ Pencil

✓ Fine-tipped scissors

✓ Patterned papers in complementary colors, 12-in. by 12-in. sheets (for letters in name)

✓ 2-in. foam or bristle paintbrush

✓ Decoupage medium in matte or satin finish

✓ Rickrack in a complementary color to wrap around perimeter of stool top (optional)

PERSONALIZED STEP STOOL

 coordinated set of scrapbook papers served as inspiration for this decoupaged step stool. Paint colors and embellishments were matched to the papers and the papers themselves vibrantly personalize this easy project. The stool is truly multifunctional and indispensable in a child's bathroom or bedroom.

1. Lightly sand the step stool to remove any varnish and wipe away the dust with a damp rag. Coat the step stool with a thin layer of primer and allow it to dry for the time recommended by the manufacturer.

2. Mask the top edge of the step stool with painters' tape then apply two thin coats of latex paint to the legs, allowing drying time between coats. Once the paint is fully dry (according to the manufacturer's recommendations), remove the tape from the top edge and mask the bottom of the step stool with tape; then paint the top of the step stool with two coats of the second color. Allow the paint to dry thoroughly between coats as well as after the second coat.

3. In the meantime, create a template for each letter in the child's name using your computer or by drawing the letters freehand

directly onto the cardstock. Be creative—vary the font and size of each letter such as in the sample shown. Print out one letter at a time onto a sheet of cardstock, if you're getting them from an online source. Then cut out the letters and use them as your templates. With the letters placed in reverse, trace them onto the wrong side of the patterned paper and cut them out.

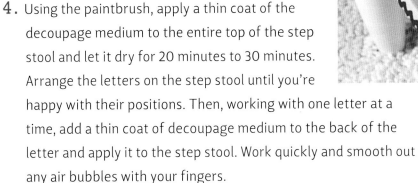

4. Using the paintbrush, apply a thin coat of the decoupage medium to the entire top of the step stool and let it dry for 20 minutes to 30 minutes. Arrange the letters on the step stool until you're happy with their positions. Then, working with one letter at a time, add a thin coat of decoupage medium to the back of the letter and apply it to the step stool. Work quickly and smooth out any air bubbles with your fingers.

5. Cut a length of rickrack, if desired, long enough to circle the top of the step stool. Brush a coat of decoupage medium along the top edge of the stool and apply the rickrack. Let it dry for 20 minutes to 30 minutes.

6. Coat the top of the step stool (over the paper letters) and the top edge of the step stool (over the rickrack) with one or two coats of decoupage medium, allowing 20 minutes to 30 minutes of drying time between coats.

✓ Scrap paper (such as butcher paper or kraft paper)

✓ 2-qt. galvanized tin bucket (the one shown here is 5½ in. tall and the top diameter is 6⅛ in.)

✓ Spray primer

✓ Spray paint in the color of your choice

✓ 2-in. foam brush

✓ Decoupage medium in matte, satin, or gloss finish

✓ Bath Bucket Top & Bottom Templates (p. 160)

✓ Pencil

✓ Patterned scrapbook paper, 12-in. by 12-in. sheets (one each of two different yet complementary designs)

✓ Paper scissors

✓ 20-in. narrow grosgrain ribbon or rickrack

✓ Water-based polyurethane

BATH BUCKET

help keep Baby's bath supplies handy in this decorative yet practical tin bucket. Decoupage medium and a top coat of polyurethane act as a moisture-resistant sealer, allowing this bucket to make its home in the splashiest of bathrooms, while adding a cheerful element that's sweet but not too babyish.

1. Make sure your work area is open and well ventilated, then prime the interior and exterior of the bucket with one or two light coats of spray primer, allowing 15 minutes to 20 minutes of drying time between coats.

2. Follow the primer with two light coats of spray paint on both the interior and exterior of the bucket, allowing 20 minutes of drying time between coats. Set the bucket aside and allow it to dry fully according to the paint manufacturer's recommendations.

3. Using the brush, seal the exterior of the bucket with a light coat of decoupage medium. Let it dry for 20 minutes to 30 minutes.

4. While the decoupage medium is drying, enlarge the Bath Bucket Top & Bottom Templates as directed and trace them onto the back of the scrapbook papers, with the narrow template on one

patterned paper and the wider template on the other. Make a set of two traced templates on each sheet, so that you have two wide and two narrow strips. Cut out the templates along the trace lines.

5. When the bucket is dry, brush decoupage medium onto the back of one of the narrow strips of paper and wrap it around the top, starting at the side seam of the bucket; the strip will circle the bucket only halfway. Smooth out any air bubbles with your fingers, working from the center out. Repeat with the second narrow strip, wrapping it around the remainder of the bucket. The seams should slightly overlap the first strip of paper.

6. Repeat this process with the wider sheets of paper for the lower half of the bucket, working out any air bubbles with your fingers and again overlapping the seams.

7. Apply a light coat of decoupage medium to the entire exterior of the bucket and adhere the thin strip of ribbon or rickrack where the papers meet. Do this before the decoupage medium dries, then allow 20 minutes to 30 minutes of drying time.

8. Add an additional coat of decoupage medium over the exterior of the bucket and let it dry thoroughly, according to the manufacturer's instructions.

9. Once the decoupage medium has dried, finish both the exterior and the interior of the bucket with a coat of water-based polyurethane (applied with a clean brush) to protect it from moisture.

Trade Secret

When working with patterns such as plaids or stripes, the best results are obtained by placing the template across the page diagonally instead of up and down or side to side. If in doubt, hold the paper up to a light (with the template behind it) so you can see exactly what the finished pattern will look like once the template is cut out.

Is for
Embellished Clothing

Lilliputian baby clothes are always a source of delight and wonder. Contribute to baby's first wardrobe with basic clothing jazzed up with one-of-a-kind personality. Right off the bat, Baby will be the coolest kid on the block!

TOOLS & MATERIALS

✓ Solid-color onesies

✓ Fabric scraps in contrasting colors and patterns to onesies

✓ Mild detergent, such as Woolite®

✓ Onesie Appliqués (p. 161) or clip art designs

✓ Cardstock for making templates

✓ Pen

✓ 1/8-in. mini hole punch

✓ Fine-tipped scissors

✓ Iron and ironing board

✓ HeatnBond® Ultrahold iron-on adhesive

APPLIQUÉD ONESIES

 abies can never have too many onesies during their first few months of life, but there's no reason they have to be boring. It only takes a few scraps of fabric and a little imagination to make an entire set of these custom clothes for your little one or for a grateful new mom.

1. Prewash all fabric scraps and onesies with a mild detergent (no fabric softeners) and dry.

2. Meanwhile, enlarge the Onesie Appliqués as directed, print them out on cardstock, and cut them out. (If you're using clip art images, do the same.)

3. After your fabric scraps are dry, iron them to remove any wrinkles, using the appropriate temperature setting for your fabric.

4. Cut the iron-on adhesive into pieces that are the same size as your fabric scraps. To adhere the iron-on adhesive to your fabrics, lower the iron to the silk setting (no steam), then place the iron-on adhesive, paper side up, on the wrong side of the fabric. Hold the iron on the adhesive paper for 2 seconds. If necessary, reposition the iron and repeat until the entire surface is bonded. Allow the fabrics to cool to the touch.

5. Place the templates in reverse on the paper side of the cooled, bonded fabric and trace around them with a pen. Cut along the trace lines with the scissors and use the mini hole punch to embellish, if desired.

6. Once the onesies are dry, iron them to remove wrinkles. Remove the paper backing from the bonded fabric pieces and arrange them on the front of the onesies as desired. Again, using a dry iron, preheated to the silk setting, hold the iron on the fabric pieces for 8 seconds to 10 seconds. Repeat, if necessary, slightly overlapping the previously bonded area until the entire fabric area has been pressed.

After-Care

For best results after embellishing, wash the onesies inside out on the delicate cycle with cold water and tumble dry on the delicate cycle with low heat. Don't dry clean.

Appliqué Inspiration

Want to come up with your own designs? Use children's books for inspiration or draw simple shapes freehand. If you're looking for something more elaborate, check out Web sites like www.clipart.com for inspiration or actual templates to download. Another option is to purchase inexpensive, oversized foam stamps from your local craft store. Stamp them on a piece of paper and cut out each section of the image to create template pieces.

Here are some ideas to get you started:

- Ladybug, butterfly, dragonfly, caterpillar, bee
- Giraffe, monkey, elephant, lion
- Cow, chick, pig, lamb
- Cherries, pumpkin, pear, apple
- Sun, moon, star
- Train, plane, truck
- A grouping of seasonal elements

✓ Side snap tees

✓ Mild detergent, such as Woolite

✓ ¼-in. grosgrain ribbon, elastic trim, or decorative piping, 1 yd. for each tee

✓ Fabric scissors

✓ Iron and ironing board

✓ Fabri-Tac

✓ Small bows (optional)

✓ Needle and thread (optional)

EMBELLISHED TEES

 nexpensive trim helps these little tees transcend their utilitarian look without taking away from their usefulness.

1. Prewash the tees and ribbon or trim to remove sizing. (This will also allow the Fabri-Tac to fully penetrate the fabrics and keep your trim securely adhered during frequent washings.) Once dry, iron the tees and ribbon/trim to remove any wrinkles.

2. *Tee with grosgrain ribbon:* Working with one small section at a time, apply Fabri-Tac to the back of the grosgrain ribbon, making sure it covers the entire surface. Starting at the front, bottom edge of the tee, glue the ribbon to the seam, following the seam line around the tee so that you end at the other bottom edge. Trim any excess ribbon and apply a small bit of glue to the cut edge so it doesn't fray. If desired, embellish the tee with small bows, stitching them securely to the tee with a needle and thread.

3. *Tee with elastic trim or piping:* Apply Fabri-Tac to the flat area of the elastic or piping, one small section at a time (because the glue dries quickly), up to the start of the decorative edge. Working from the front, bottom edge of the tee, glue the trim or piping to the inside of the seam, around the tee's edge on the inside of the shirt. Trim the excess at the other bottom edge and glue it securely.

Just Your Style

Search through sewing and trimming stores for unusual buttons and premade appliqués to make a simple set of onesies, perhaps one for each day of the week. A few hand stitches are all it takes to pull together this simple project.

Buttons: Place buttons at the top of the onesies and stitch them in place, making sure the buttons are tightly secured. *Safety note:* Choose small buttons that can be securely stitched to the onesie. Larger buttons allow baby to grab onto them, increasing the risk of them being pulled off.

Appliqués: If desired, use a bit of Fabri-Tac to hold the appliqué in place on the onesie. Go back with the needle and thread and make small stitches around the edge of the appliqué to secure it in place.

Is for First Shoes

You can't help but marvel at how small a newborn's feet are. Help keep Baby's tiny tootsies warm with these adorable shoes crafted from wool felt for extra durability.

TOOLS & MATERIALS

- ✓ Sole Template (p. 162)
- ✓ Shoe Template #1 (p. 162)
- ✓ Pencil
- ✓ Fine-tipped scissors
- ✓ Solid-color wool felt, 9-in. by 12-in. piece (one sheet for each pair of shoes)
- ✓ Disappearing-ink pen
- ✓ Fabric scissors
- ✓ Scalloped-edge scissors (optional)
- ✓ 1/16-in. hole punch
- ✓ Four 1/8-in. eyelets
- ✓ Eyelet setter and setting mat
- ✓ Small hammer for setting eyelets
- ✓ Sewing machine
- ✓ Thread to match felt
- ✓ Straight pins
- ✓ 1/4-in. or narrower ribbon (24-in. for each pair)

RIBBON-TRIMMED SHOES

 resto chango! Give a mom the gift of choice with shoes that can be dressed up or down with the mere switch of a ribbon. Make a pair of shoes in a neutral color and present them along with an assortment of different patterned and textured ribbons for versatility.

1. Get a measurement of Baby's foot and enlarge the Sole Template by a percentage that ends up measuring 1/2 in. to 3/4 in. longer than Baby's foot. Enlarge Shoe Template #1 by the same percentage and cut out both templates along the trace lines. Place the templates on the wool felt and trace around them using the disappearing-ink pen. Cut them out along the trace lines.

2. If desired, trim the inside edge of the shoe cutout with the scalloped-edge scissors and punch a hole in each scallop with the 1/16-in. hole punch for decorative effect.

3. Punch two holes in the shoe cutout (see the template for placement) with the 1/16-in. hole punch and push a 1/8-in. eyelet through each hole. Turn the shoe cutout over and set the eyelets

with the small hammer and setting mat (see "Trade Secrets," at right).

4. With the wrong side of the shoe cutout facing up, fold it in half lengthwise so the straight edges meet. Sew the back seam together using a straight stitch, 1/8 in. from the edge. This will be the heel.

5. With the shoe still inside out, use straight pins to temporarily attach the top of the shoe to the sole, matching the edges. (See "Making Shoes," on p. 19.)

6. Again using a straight stitch, attach the sole by sewing around the shoe, 1/4 in. from the edge. Trim the excess threads and trim the felt closely around the seam.

7. Turn the shoe right side out and shape it with your fingers from the inside out.

8. Repeat Steps 1 through 7 for the second shoe.

9. To complete the shoes, thread 12 in. of ribbon through the eyelet holes in each shoe. Tie the ribbon in a knot or bow once the shoe is on Baby's foot. Trim the excess ribbon as needed.

Trade Secret

Need some help setting eyelets? Just follow these simple steps:

1. Place your setting mat on a hard, flat surface, such as a countertop or an uncarpeted floor.

2. Place the felt cutout, right side down, on the setting mat with the back of the eyelet facing up through the hole.

3. Center the eyelet setter with the middle of the "flower" (the shape of the end of your eyelet setter) inserted into the back of the eyelet.

4. Tap the eyelet setter with the small hammer two or three times, until the eyelet splits. (The set eyelet will curl, resembling a flower when you're done.)

5. Turn the felt right side up.

- ✓ Sole Template (p. 163)
- ✓ Shoe Template #1 (p. 163)
- ✓ Strap Template (p.163)
- ✓ Pencil
- ✓ Fine-tipped scissors
- ✓ Solid-color wool felt, 9-in. by 12-in. piece (one for each pair of shoes)
- ✓ Disappearing-ink pen
- ✓ Fabric scissors
- ✓ Sewing machine
- ✓ Thread to match felt
- ✓ Straight pins
- ✓ 2 sets of small sew-on snaps for straps
- ✓ Needle
- ✓ Flowers templates (p.163)
- ✓ Contrasting wool felt for floral embellishment, approximately 2 in. by 4 in.
- ✓ Fabri-Tac or other quick-setting fabric glue

CLASSIC MARY JANES

 S pecifically for little ladies, the addition of a strap turns the basic shoe into a classic Mary Jane. A floral embellishment adds a touch of fun to the simple design.

1. Get a measurement of baby's foot and enlarge the Sole Template by a percentage that ends up measuring $1/2$ in. to $3/4$ in. longer than Baby's foot. Enlarge the Shoe Template #1 and Strap Template by the same percentage and cut out all templates along the trace lines. Place the templates on the wool felt and trace around them using the disappearing-ink pen. Cut them out on the trace lines.

2. With the wrong side facing up, fold the shoe cutout in half lengthwise so the straight edges meet. Sew the back seam together using a straight stitch, $1/8$ in. from the edge. This will be the heel.

3. With the shoe still inside out, pin the strap to one side of the shoe for placement (where the eyelet hole would normally be made) and use a straight stitch to attach it to the shoe.

4. Again, with the shoe still inside out, temporarily pin the top of the shoe to the sole, matching the edges.

5. Using a straight stitch, attach the sole by sewing around the shoe, ¼ in. from the edge. Trim the excess threads and trim the felt closely around the seam.

6. Turn the shoe right side out and shape it with your fingers from the inside out.

7. Hand-sew one side of the snap to the loose end of the shoe strap and the other side of the snap to the side of the shoe.

8. Repeat steps 1 through 7 for the second shoe, but sew the shoe strap on the opposite side from that of the first shoe.

9. Cut out both of the Flowers Templates and place them on the contrasting wool felt. Trace two copies of the flower elements onto the felt with the disappearing-ink pen and cut them out with the fine-tipped scissors. Use Fabri-Tac to glue the flower embellishments to the toe of each shoe, layering the two pieces as shown above.

✓ Sole Template (p. 163)

✓ Shoe Template #2 (p. 163)

✓ Shoe Panel Template (p. 163)

✓ Pencil

✓ Solid-color wool felt, 9-in. by 12-in. piece (one piece for each pair of shoes)

✓ Disappearing-ink pen

✓ Fabri-Tac or other quick-setting fabric glue

✓ Fabric scissors

✓ Pinking shears (optional)

✓ 1/16-in. hole punch

✓ Four 1/8-in. eyelets

✓ Eyelet setter & setting mat

✓ Small hammer for setting eyelets

✓ 1/4 in. or narrower ribbon, 24 in. for each pair

✓ Sewing machine

✓ Thread to match felt

✓ Straight pins

BOY BOOTIES

 o a little crazy with your favorite color combinations when dressing the feet of the new man in your life. A combination of fabric glue and sewing keeps this shoe project from getting complicated.

1. Get a measurement of Baby's foot and enlarge the Sole Template by a percentage that ends up measuring 1/2 in. to 3/4 in. longer than Baby's foot. Enlarge Shoe Template #2 and the Shoe Panel Template by the same percentage and cut out all the templates along the trace lines. Place the templates on the wool felt and trace around them using the disappearing-ink pen. Cut them out on the trace lines. You will need to make two wool cutouts of the Shoe Panel Template for each shoe.

2. Line up the outer edges of the two shoe panels on top of the shoe cutout and use Fabri-Tac to glue them to the top of the shoe, lining up the back seam and bottom edges of the panels to the shoe. Trim the inner edge of the shoe—use pinking shears, if desired—but do not trim the tongue of the shoe.

3. Punch a hole in each of the shoe panels (see the template for placement) with the 1/16-in. hole punch and push a 1/8-in. eyelet

through each hole. Turn the shoe panels over and set the eyelets with the small hammer and setting mat (see "Trade Secrets" on p. 55).

4. Thread 12 in. of ribbon through the eyelets and tie in a bow on the right side of the shoe cutout. Trim any excess ribbon as desired.

5. With the shoe inside out, fold the shoe cutout in half lengthwise so that straight edges meet. Sew together the back seam using a straight stitch, 1/8 in. from the edge. This will be the heel.

6. With the shoe still inside out, temporarily pin the top of the shoe to the sole for placement, matching the edges.

7. Using a straight stitch, attach the sole by sewing around the shoe 1/4 in. from the edge. Trim the excess threads and trim the felt closely around the seam.

8. Turn the shoe right side out and shape it with your fingers, from the inside out.

9. Repeat steps 1 through 8 for the second shoe.

Is for
Growth Chart

Babies grow up to be children in no time!
Mark their rapid progress on this colorful giraffe,
who also keeps a watchful eye over your little one.

TOOLS & MATERIALS

- ✓ Patterned cotton fabric, 1⅔ yd.
- ✓ Medium-weight canvas, 2 yd.
- ✓ Iron and ironing board
- ✓ Giraffe Template (p. 163)
- ✓ Kraft paper for making template
- ✓ Pencil
- ✓ Scotch® tape
- ✓ Paper scissors
- ✓ HeatnBond Ultrahold iron-on adhesive, 1⅔ yd.
- ✓ Fabric scissors
- ✓ FrayBlock™ or Fray Check™
- ✓ Felt in a complementary color, 1 yd.
- ✓ Yardstick
- ✓ White pencil or disappearing-ink pen
- ✓ Rub-on transfer numbers 2 through 5 (found with scrapbooking supplies)
- ✓ Wooden craft stick
- ✓ Fabri-Tac or other fabric glue
- ✓ Scraps of white and black felt
- ✓ ⅝-in. ribbon, 2 yd.
- ✓ Fine-tipped textile marker (optional)

1. Prewash and dry all fabric then iron it to remove wrinkles.

2. Enlarge the Giraffe Template as directed, copying different sections of it onto several large sheets of paper. Tape the sheets together to form a continuous template and cut it out along the trace lines.

3. Preheat your iron to the silk setting. Turn the patterned fabric wrong side up and place the iron-on adhesive on top of it, paper side up (try to line up the edges as best you can). Fuse the adhesive to the fabric by pressing sections with the iron, 1 second to 2 seconds in each area. Set it aside to cool.

4. Place the Giraffe template, in reverse, on top of the paper side of the fused fabric. (This is easiest when done on a hard floor or tabletop.) Trace around the template with a pencil and cut it out along the trace lines with fabric scissors. Set it aside.

5. Cut the canvas into a 20-in. by 58-in. rectangle. Treat the edges with FrayBlock or Fray Check to keep the ends from unraveling or fraying (an alternative is to hem all the edges on a sewing machine with a ¼-in. seam). Set it aside to dry for 15 minutes to 20 minutes.

6. While your canvas is drying, cut a strip from the colored felt that measures 36 in. by 2¼ in. Line it up against a yardstick and make marks on one side at 1-in. intervals with either a white pencil or disappearing-ink pen. Make 1¾-in. cuts in the felt at each 1-in. interval with the fabric scissors to make a fringe.

7. Using the rub-on transfer numbers, apply the number 2 at the first line by placing it on the felt, and rubbing over it with a wooden craft stick on a hard surface. Count up 1 ft. then apply a number 3. Continue counting up 1 ft. each for the numbers 4 and 5.

8. Preheat the iron to the silk setting. Remove the paper backing from the fabric giraffe and place it on the canvas in the desired position. Fuse the fabric to the canvas by holding the iron over each section of fabric for approximately 10 seconds (you may need even more pressing time since canvas is a heavy fabric). Start at one end and work your way to the other, until all the fabric has been fused.

9. Apply a line of fabric glue to the solid edge of the felt fringe and glue it parallel to the giraffe's neck.

10. Make an eye from the scraps of black and white felt, using the template as a guide. Cut solid pieces from the colored felt to line the ears. Attach all embellishments with fabric glue.

11. Use more fabric glue to adhere a 1-yd. piece of ribbon to the top corners of the growth chart so it can be hung. Cover the ends with a border of ribbon glued over the top and bottom edges of the chart.

12. To hang the chart, measure 2 ft. up from the floor and align the first notch on the giraffe's fringe with that 2-ft. mark. If desired, measurements and dates can be permanently marked directly on the canvas with a fine-tipped textile marker.

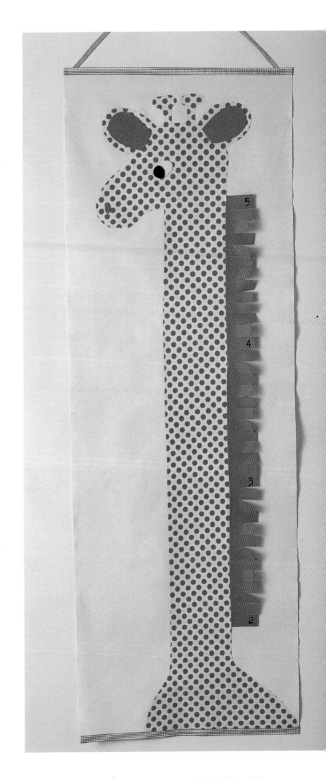

Is for Hangers

New babies get lots of clothing. Give them the royal treatment with sets of personalized or decorative hangers. They're a cinch to make, and nothing could be sweeter.

TOOLS & MATERIALS

✓ Child-size wooden hangers

✓ Fine-grade sandpaper

✓ Masking tape

✓ Scrap paper

✓ Water-based spray primer

✓ Water-based spray paint in desired color

✓ Computer-generated monogram, clip art, or hand-drawn monogram

✓ EZ Crafts Pressure-fax® transfer pen and paper (or similar product)

✓ Paper scissors

✓ Scotch tape (optional)

✓ Spoon or other burnishing tool, such as a bone folder

✓ Extra fine-tipped paint pen in desired color for monogram

✓ Spray acrylic sealer in matte finish

✓ Decorative ribbon, ⅓ yd. for each hanger

✓ Craft glue (optional)

MONOGRAMMED HANGERS

 ake it personal with a suite of monogrammed hangers destined to become an instant heirloom. Transfer paper and a fine-tipped paint pen allow beginners to get professional-looking results with ease.

1. Lightly sand the hangers to remove any lacquer and then wipe them clean with a dry rag. Cover the hooks with masking tape to avoid getting paint on them. Apply a thin layer of primer on one side of the hangers; let dry for 20 minutes to 30 minutes and repeat on the other side.

2. Once the hangers are dry to the touch, spray them with two coats of spray paint, allowing the first coat to dry for 20 minutes to 30 minutes before adding the second coat. Let the hangers dry fully, according to the manufacturer's instructions, before proceeding.

3. Make a transfer using your monogram and the transfer pen and paper. If your monogram is computer generated, print out the monogram as a mirror, or reverse, image. (If your printer software doesn't have a mirror setting, print your monogram on a piece of vellum or other translucent paper that allows you to trace the monogram on the backside of the paper.) If you're using a hand-drawn or clip art monogram, the image will also need to

be traced in reverse so that when it's applied to the hanger, the initial will be transferred properly. Cut out a piece of transfer paper slightly larger than your monogram and place it over your monogram. Use the transfer pen to trace over the monogram (remember, the resulting monogram should be backward).

4. Turn the transfer, ink-side down, onto the surface of your hanger in the desired location. Add a piece of masking or Scotch tape over the back of the transfer paper to hold it in place. Rub firmly over the transfer paper with the back of a spoon or other burnishing tool to transfer the image to the hanger. Use the tape as a hinge to lift the paper up on one side (without removing it) and check to see that the image has fully transferred. If not, reposition the paper and rub over it again. Remove the transfer paper and set it aside (most transfers can be used a couple of times).

5. Use the fine-tipped paint pen to trace over the transferred image, filling in all desired areas with the paint. Allow the monogram to dry thoroughly, according to the instructions on the paint pen.

6. Spray the hanger with two light coats of acrylic sealer, allowing 15 minutes to 20 minutes of dry time between coats.

7. Remove the masking tape from the hook and tie a bow around the top for embellishment. If desired, add some craft glue to the bottom of the bow to secure it to the hanger.

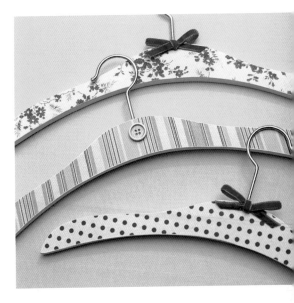

Just Your Style

If you have leftover scrapbook paper or wallpaper from baby's room, transform ordinary hangers in a snap.

Follow the instructions for the monogrammed hanger to sand and paint the hangers. Trace each hanger onto the paper side of a PEELnSTICK double-sided adhesive sheet and cut it out. Remove the shiny side of the adhesive and adhere it to the wrong side of the patterned paper, then cut it out. Finally, remove the paper backing from the patterned paper and attach it to the hanger. Sand the edges with an emery board and seal the hanger with spray acrylic sealer. Embellish the hanger as desired.

TOOLS & MATERIALS

- ✓ Child-size wooden hangers
- ✓ Fine-grade sandpaper
- ✓ Masking tape
- ✓ Scrap paper
- ✓ Water-based spray primer
- ✓ Water-based spray paint in desired color
- ✓ Decorative rubber stamps
- ✓ Colored pigment or solvent dye ink pads
- ✓ Scrap paper
- ✓ Stamp cleaner
- ✓ Spray acrylic sealer in a matte finish (optional)
- ✓ Decorative ribbon for embellishment, ⅓ yd. for each hanger (optional)

RUBBER-STAMPED HANGERS

 hese practical yet decorative child-size hangers get a makeover with a handful of rubber stamps and colorful ink pads. Even if you have no experience with rubber stamping, these small delights can be whipped up in an afternoon.

1. Lightly sand the hangers to remove any lacquer and then wipe them clean with a dry rag. Cover the hooks with masking tape to avoid getting paint on them. Apply a thin layer of primer on one side of the hangers; let dry for 20 minutes to 30 minutes and repeat on the other side.

2. Once the hangers are dry to the touch, spray them with two coats of spray paint, allowing the first coat to dry for 20 minutes to 30 minutes before adding the second coat. Let the hangers dry fully, according to the manufacturer's instructions, before proceeding.

3. Once the hangers are dry, embellish them with rubber stamps. For opaque designs, add ink to the stamp each time you use it. For a faded, vintage quality, add ink to the stamp and lightly press it onto scrap paper to remove excess ink before stamping

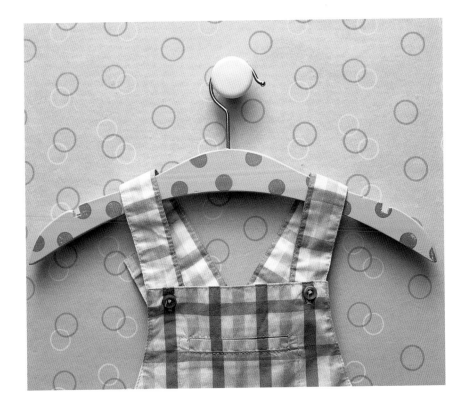

Trade Secret

Pigment dye ink pads are typically used when stamping on porous surfaces because the ink won't thoroughly dry on a painted wood surface. However, you can still use these readily available inks if you spray your finished hangers with several coats of acrylic sealer after stamping (although you should still allow the ink to dry for at least several hours or overnight before spraying with the sealer).

If you're using solvent dye ink pads, meant for surfaces such as rubber, painted wood, or leather, the results will be permanent once dry and won't require a sealer (although sealers help keep paint from chipping). See Resources on p. 171 for more information on solvent dye ink pads.

on the hanger. Practice beforehand on scrap paper to determine the look you want. (If you're using pigment ink, mistakes can be wiped away with a damp paper towel. Solvent inks are permanent immediately.)

4. When you are satisfied with your designs, clean the stamps with stamp cleaner and let the ink on the hangers dry. Generally, the ink will look dry when it is.

5. If you used pigment inks, let the hangers dry for a few hours, then spray them with several light coats of acrylic sealer, allowing 15 minutes to 20 minutes between coats. Let the last coat of sealer dry for 20 minutes, then remove the masking tape from the hook and tie a bow around the top for embellishment, if desired

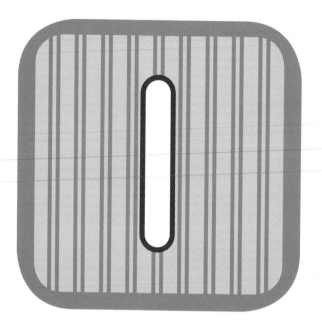

Is for Iron-on Transfer Pillow

Turn a cherished first photo of Baby into a keepsake pillow with the simplicity of iron-on transfer paper. Readily available and easy to use, it's great for customizing other fabric items, too, such as a tote or diaper bag.

John Peter D'Emilia

TOOLS & MATERIALS

- ✓ Light-color cotton fabric, ⅓ yd.
- ✓ Iron and ironing board
- ✓ Rotary cutter
- ✓ Cutting mat
- ✓ Ruler
- ✓ Computer and color inkjet printer
- ✓ Digital or scanned photo (saved in jpg format)
- ✓ Iron-on T-shirt transfer paper, 8½-in. by 11-in. sheet
- ✓ Pillowcase (of any flat material)
- ✓ Hard, smooth, heat-resistant surface
- ✓ Scissors
- ✓ Straight pins
- ✓ Rickrack, 2 yd. (optional)
- ✓ Sewing machine and thread to match fabric color
- ✓ Fiberfill for pillow
- ✓ Medium-size needle for hand sewing

1. Prewash and dry the fabric, then iron to remove any wrinkles.

2. Using the rotary cutter on the cutting mat, cut two 11½-in. by 14-in. pieces of fabric for the pillow; set them aside.

3. Using the computer, resize your photograph if needed (the one shown measures 5½ in. by 7½ in.). Add Baby's name to your pillow using a word-processing program, if desired (see "Computer Tutor" on p. 15).

4. Once the layout is complete, place a sheet of iron-on transfer paper in your printer and print the image in reverse, or in the "mirror" mode. (If "iron-on transfer paper" shows up in your drop-down print menu, select it and the image will automatically print in reverse.) For best results, print your photo on the highest quality setting and let it dry for a few minutes before handling.

5. While the print is drying, preheat the iron to its highest temperature setting (without steam). Let it heat up for 5 minutes before proceeding.

6. Fold the pillowcase in half, so the short edges meet, and place it on the heat-resistant surface (not an ironing board) with the seam of the pillowcase hanging over the edge. Iron it to remove any wrinkles. Place one of the pillow fabric pieces, right side up, on the center of the folded pillowcase.

7. Use the scissors to trim around the image and text to be transferred, leaving a ⅛-in. border (this area will transfer clear).

8. Place the transfer sheet face-down and center it on the pillow fabric. Use both hands to hold the iron and apply firm, downward pressure for approximately 3 minutes, continuously moving the iron in a circle over the transfer, keeping the pressure constant. With the pressure still firm, slowly iron from one side of the transfer to the other, overlapping passes and making sure all the edges have been pressed. Let the transfer cool to the touch.

9. Once the transfer paper has cooled, slowly remove it, starting with one corner. If you find that the corners or the edges of your transfer begin to lift when you pull up the paper, replace the ironing paper as it was and reheat the transfer for 1 minute, focusing on the corners and edges.

10. With the right sides of the pillow fabric pieces facing, pin around the perimeter with straight pins, lining up the edges as best you can. If you're using rickrack, pin it between the layers of fabric with the edge of the rickrack flush with the edge of the pillow fabric.

11. On the sewing machine, sew a straight stitch around the edges of the pillow fabric, with a $\frac{1}{4}$-in. seam. Leave 4 in. or 5 in. open on one side and turn the pillow right side out.

12. Stuff the pillow with fiberfill until the desired fullness has been achieved. Hand-sew the opening closed, turning the edges in before stitching.

John Peter D'Emilia

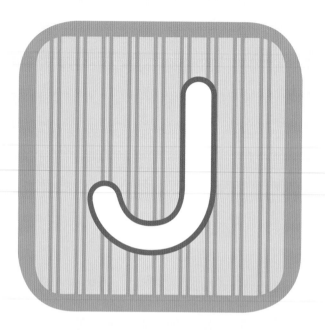

Is for Journal

These small, accordion albums are the perfect place to record the milestones
of Baby's first year. Fill the journal with photographs taken each month,
handprints that grow progressively larger, a collection of notes that detail Baby's firsts,
or a delightful combination of both visual and written memories.

Benjamin

4 months

1 month

- ✓ Bookboard, enough to cut two 5-in. by 7-in. boards
- ✓ Cutting mat
- ✓ Drawing or artists' paper, 38-in. long
- ✓ Heavy-duty craft or utility knife
- ✓ Ruler
- ✓ Bone folder
- ✓ Decorative art paper, enough to cut two 7-in. by 9-in. pieces
- ✓ Scrap paper
- ✓ Pencil
- ✓ Yes! paste or a PVA adhesive made for bookbinding
- ✓ Paste brush
- ✓ Fabri-Tac or other quick-setting fabric glue
- ✓ Decorative ribbon in a complementary color, 5½-in.
- ✓ Heavy weights (or heavy stack of books)
- ✓ Cardstock for nameplate, large enough to fit in your printer if using a computer
- ✓ Computer and printer (optional)
- ✓ Fountain or calligraphy pen (optional)
- ✓ 2 small buttons

PAPER-COVERED JOURNAL

 t's simple to make your own customized journals, and they can be addictive once you start. With all the wonderful varieties of paper on the market, don't be surprised if you suddenly find yourself with a journal for every year of your baby's childhood!

1. Place the bookboard onto the cutting mat and use the craft or utility knife to cut it into two 5-in. by 7-in. pieces. (See "Finding the Grain," on p. 79, before cutting the boards or paper for the journal.)

2. Cut the drawing or artists' paper into a 6¾-in. by 38-in. strip using the craft knife. (For more information on artists' paper see "Trade Secret," on p. 79.) Line up your ruler vertically 4¾ in. from the short edge and use the bone folder to score a folding line in the paper, following the ruler's edge. Fold the paper to the right along the scored line.

3. Continue scoring lines with the bone folder along each folded edge as you fold the paper back and forth in accordion fashion

until you've reached the end of the paper strip. Set it aside. (See "Making a Journal," on p. 20.)

4. Trim the decorative paper into two 7-in. by 9-in. pieces. On a flat surface, lay one piece of paper facedown on scrap paper. Center one of the bookboard panels on the paper and trace around the board with a pencil. Remove the board and trim the paper corners on a diagonal, leaving enough paper to cover the corners of the board. (See "Making a Journal," on p. 20.)

5. Brush a thin coat of Yes! paste or PVA adhesive onto the back of the decorative paper, extending just past the trace lines. Place the bookboard panel on the decorative paper, lining up the edges with the trace lines. Turn the board over and smooth out any air bubbles with the bone folder.

6. Turn the board face down again, and brush more paste onto one of the long edges of the decorative paper and fold it over the bookboard edge, making sure the paper is pulled taut and lies flat. Repeat on the other long side.

Just Your Style

There are plenty of premade embellishments that make decorating your journal easy. This journal features a metal label holder (adhered with Perfect Glue 1) and a rub-on alphabet letter. All the other steps are the same as the paper-covered journal.

Just Your Style

Lots of papers, whether handmade or machine made, make excellent bookbinding papers. The most important thing to look for is paper that's flexible (if it's too stiff it's hard to work with) and that isn't too thick (or your corners and folds will be bulky). Sheets of gift wrap with a matte finish can work just as well as art papers. Check Resources, on pp. 171–172, for more paper options and where to get them. (Don't be afraid to ask specific questions about a paper before ordering by telephone or online.)

7. Use the tip of the bone folder to fold in the corners of the paper at the top and bottom of the bookboard piece (creating clean, tight corners when the paper is folded, as if you were wrapping a gift). Apply more paste to the short edges and fold them over the bookboard panel, smoothing with the bone folder if necessary.

8. Repeat Steps 4 through 7 for the second piece of bookboard and decorative paper.

9. Apply a thin line of Fabri-Tac or other fabric glue to the back of the decorative ribbon and glue it horizontally across the middle to top-middle of the front of one of the bookboard panels. Bring the edges of the ribbon over the bookboard sides and glue them to the back of the bookboard panel.

10. Place a piece of scrap paper between the first and second page of your accordion-folded paper and brush a thin layer of paste on the entire surface of the top page, working from the center and extending just past the edges. Remove the scrap paper and adhere the accordion panel vertically to the inside of the ribbon-covered board, centering it. Smooth over the paper with the bone folder and make sure the edges are securely adhered.

11. Repeat Step 10 with the second piece of bookboard and the other end of the accordion-folded paper.

12. Wrap the book in scrap paper and place it on a flat surface under heavy weights or a stack of books until it dries completely, about 8 hours or overnight.

Finding the Grain

It's important when making books that the grain of the bookboard and papers are all parallel to each other. This way they pull in one direction, as opposed to working against each other and leading to a permanently warped final product.

Finding a bookboard's grain is easiest when the board is larger than 5 in. by 7 in. To find the grain, hold the board at the opposing edges and gently pull them toward you until the board begins to curve slightly in its center. Repeat by pulling in the opposite sides in the same fashion. The board will have more give and will bend more easily when you're bending it with the grain.

Once you know the direction of the bookboard's grain, find the paper's grain by bringing two of its opposing edges together and lightly pressing the palm of your hand along the rolled area opposite the two edges. Unfold and repeat with the opposite edges, again lightly pressing with your hand. The direction with more give is the direction of the grain.

When assembling your accordion folded paper, cut the paper so that the fold lines run parallel with the grain. Decorative papers that cover the bookboards, as well as the bookboards themselves, should be cut so the grain runs top to bottom.

Trade Secret

Artists' paper is available in very long lengths, and while it's best to use a continuous length of paper, you can work with shorter papers if you don't have access to the length indicated in the materials list or don't want to order it from an online source.

Mask all but $1/2$ in. of one edge of your paper with a piece of scrap paper. Brush paste on the edge of the paper and place another piece of paper over it. Rub the edge with your bone folder until it adheres. Continue adding lengths of paper until you reach the desired length, then accordion-fold as directed.

13. Meanwhile, make a nameplate for the cover of the journal using cardstock and either a computer or a fountain or calligraphy pen. Trim the card to measure $1\frac{1}{2}$ in. wide by $2\frac{1}{4}$ in. long. Use fabric glue to adhere the card to the front of the journal, centering the nameplate on the ribbon. Use more fabric glue to adhere a button to each side of the nameplate.

Is for
Keepsake Box

Even with the best intentions, baby mementos often end up in a box. So make it a keepsake box, and even your storage will have style! These quick transformations are easy to whip up and perfect for housing priceless little treasures.

✓ Patterned cotton fabric for base (you may wish to make templates first to determine the amount of fabric needed)

✓ Patterned cotton fabric in complementary color for lid

✓ Iron and ironing board

✓ Unfinished wooden box with a loose-fitting lid and no hinges (the box shown here is 8½ in. by 12 in. by 4 in.)

✓ Kraft paper for templates (and to cover work surface)

✓ Pencil

✓ Tape measure

✓ Ruler

✓ Scissors

✓ Disappearing-ink pen

✓ Rotary cutter

✓ Cutting mat

✓ Yes! paste

✓ Paste brush

✓ Fabri-Tac, or other quick-setting fabric glue

✓ Ribbon or other embellishment for box (optional)

FABRIC-COVERED WOODEN BOX

The softness of fabric belies the sturdiness of this wooden box, customized to hold all of your special keepsakes. You'll find these versatile and easy-to-make storage boxes not only useful for mementos but for many other items in the nursery as well.

1. Iron the fabric to remove any wrinkles.

2. Make templates for both the box base and the box lid (see "Box Templates," on p. 18). Place the base of the box (without the lid) on the kraft paper; trace around it with a pencil, then remove it from the kraft paper. Using the tape measure, measure the sides of the box, starting at the bottom edge and ending your measurement approximately ½ in. over the interior edge of the box; make note of the measurement. Line a ruler up against each trace line and extend the line from the box outline to the length of the box side measurement you recorded. Repeat for all four sides of the outline. Use scissors to cut out both templates along the trace lines (remember to cut out the squares between the line intersections at the corners).

3. Repeat the same process for the lid.

4. Place the box base and box lid templates on the wrong sides of the fabric and trace around them with a disappearing-ink pen. Trim the fabric to size with the rotary cutter on the cutting mat.

5. Brush a thin layer of Yes! paste onto the bottom of the box base and place it on the appropriate fabric, lining up the box with the trimmed edges. Turn the box over and smooth the fabric with your fingers. Once smooth, turn the box base side down again.

6. Working one side at a time, brush paste onto the sides of the box, pulling the fabric up and smoothing it with your fingers. Brush a little more paste on the outside edge of the box and just inside the interior rim of the box; adhere the fabric over the rim and smooth with your fingers. Make sure the edges of the fabric meet at each corner of the box and are securely adhered to the box.

7. Repeat Steps 5 and 6 for the box lid, but don't bring the fabric completely over the edge into the interior rim of the lid. This may make your box lid too tight and prevent it from fitting over the base. Instead, just adhere the fabric over the bottom edge of the lid. Trim the fabric with scissors if necessary.

8. Embellish the box as desired.

Is for Lampshade

Inexpensive vintage bases, easily found on online auction sites such as eBay, find a home in the present when updated with customized, fabric-covered lampshades. Requiring no special skills, the final result rivals more expensive reproductions found in chic baby boutiques.

TOOLS & MATERIALS

- ✓ Inexpensive, white clip-on lampshade (cloth or paper) in a paneled bell shape
- ✓ Kraft or butcher paper for template
- ✓ Pencil
- ✓ Paper scissors
- ✓ Lightweight to medium-weight fabric, ¼ yd., two pieces in different yet complementary colors or patterns
- ✓ Iron and ironing board
- ✓ Disappearing-ink pen
- ✓ Fabric scissors
- ✓ Yes! paste
- ✓ Paste brush
- ✓ Decorative ribbon, 1½ yd. (no wider than the panel seams on the lampshade)
- ✓ Fabri-Tac or other quick-setting fabric glue
- ✓ Bias tape in a complementary color, one package

DRESSED-UP PANELS

 wo patterns are better than one when it comes to outfitting this charming paneled shade. Bold yet sweet patterns are unified by a simple color scheme. It's a head turner that couldn't be easier to make!

1. Make a template for a paneled shade (see "Making Templates," at right, for guidance).

2. Use this template to create the required number of panels from the two complementary pieces of fabric. Trace the templates onto the fabric using the disappearing-ink pen. You will want to alternate the two fabrics on the panels. Cut along the trace lines.

3. Glue each fabric panel onto the lampshade, applying a thin coat of Yes! paste to the lampshade with a paste brush. Place the panels so they lie next to each other, overlapping the panel seams only slightly. (The decorative ribbon will hide these seams.)

4. When all the panels have been glued to the lampshade, measure and cut the ribbon to cover the length of the panel seaming. Use Fabri-Tac to attach the ribbon to each seam. Then wrap the top and bottom edges of the lampshade with the bias tape; cut it to size, unfold one edge of the tape and glue it over the exposed

Making Templates

Use this method for the classic, empire lampshade as well as the square lampshade:

1. Tape a piece of kraft or butcher paper to the existing lampshade, aligning the edge of the paper with the lampshade's original seam.
2. Pull the paper around the lampshade, smoothly, with no gaps between the paper and the lampshade. If necessary, tape on additional pieces of paper, in a patchwork fashion, until the lampshade is fully covered, with a slight overlap along the back seam. If you use more than one piece of paper, make sure all pieces are securely taped together.
3. Use a pencil to trace around the top and bottom edges of the shade, then gently remove the paper and cut along the penciled line. You will now have a paper template for your lampshade.

Paneled bell shades are a little trickier to make templates for. However, the good news is that you only need to make a template for one of the panels:

1. Tape kraft or butcher paper to one of the panels and use the side of a pencil or crayon to rub over the paper. (Paneled lampshades have wire seams that will appear darker on the paper when you rub over it with a pencil or crayon.)
2. Cut it out just outside the seam lines and check for fit on the lampshade, trimming if necessary. Use this template to make fabric cutouts to cover each lampshade panel.

lampshade edge, so that it rests on the inside of the lampshade. Glue the folded edge to the surface of the lampshade. To add definition, glue another piece of bias tape over the first layer.

TOOLS & MATERIALS

- ✓ Inexpensive, white clip-on lampshade (cloth or paper) in a classic empire shape
- ✓ Kraft or butcher paper for template
- ✓ Masking tape
- ✓ Pencil
- ✓ Paper scissors
- ✓ Lightweight to medium-weight decorative cotton or canvas fabric, ½ yd.
- ✓ Iron and ironing board
- ✓ Disappearing-ink pen
- ✓ Fabric scissors
- ✓ Yes! paste
- ✓ Paste brush
- ✓ Small craft paintbrush for detail work
- ✓ Bias tape in a complementary color, 1 package
- ✓ Fabri-Tac or other quick-setting fabric glue
- ✓ Rickrack or pompom trim, 1 yd. (optional)
- ✓ Vintage lamp base

A CLASSIC REINTERPRETED

 umpty Dumpty gets a new look with a classic gingham print spiced up in a contemporary shade of tangerine. Simple, sweet rickrack trim is always a winner in the nursery and softens the overall look of the shade.

1. Make a paper template for your lampshade (see "Making Templates," on p. 87 for guidance).

2. Iron the fabric to remove wrinkles. Lay the paper template on the right side of the fabric and trace around it with a disappearing-ink pen. Cut outside the trace line leaving 3/8 in. excess on all sides for seam allowance. Fold one edge of the straight seam back along the trace line and iron flat. This will be the overlap for the back seam.

3. Brush a thin, even coat of Yes! paste onto the lampshade with the paste brush.

4. Placing the fabric so it falls on the front of the lampshade, wrap the fabric around the shade, smoothing out any wrinkles or air bubbles with your fingers as you go. If the fabric isn't aligned on your first try, gently pull it up before the glue dries and place on the shade again.

5. Use the small craft brush to add Yes! paste along the back seam of the lampshade; be sure the material is taut and press the folded edge of the fabric flat with your hand.

6. Cut small slits in the fabric along the top and bottom of the shade, approximately 1 in. apart. Using Yes! paste and the small paintbrush, adhere the fabric to the inside edges of the lampshade.

7. Finish by gluing bias tape around the top and bottom edges of the lampshade. Unfold one edge of the tape and glue it over the exposed lampshade edge, so that it rests on the inside of the lampshade. Glue the folded edge to the surface of the lampshade. This will give a neat, clean look to your shade.

8. If desired, use Fabri-Tac or another quick-setting fabric glue to embellish the bottom edge with rickrack or pompom trim.

Preparing a vintage lamp base

Cleaning
Most vintage lamps are made from painted wood or ceramic and can be cleaned with a mild detergent and water.

Painting
If certain parts of the base need a fresh coat of paint, sand the damaged areas with fine grade sandpaper; prime and then paint. For the best result, take the lamp with you to the paint store. Most are equipped to match the paint color by computer.

Safety
To prevent shocks or burns, vintage lamps should be rewired, particularly if cords are loose or damaged. You can do this yourself (instructions are readily available online) or consult an expert at your local lighting store.

TOOLS & MATERIALS

✓ Lamp base

✓ Masking tape

✓ Spray primer

✓ Antique white spray paint

✓ Inexpensive clip-on lampshade in the shape of your choice (do not use a panel style)

✓ Kraft or butcher paper for template

✓ Pencil

✓ Paper scissors

✓ Lightweight to medium-weight cotton or canvas fabric, ½ yd.

✓ Iron and ironing board

✓ Disappearing-ink pen

✓ Fabric scissors

✓ Yes! paste

✓ Paste brush

✓ Small craft paintbrush for detail work

✓ Thin velvet ribbon in complementary color, 2 yd.

✓ Fabri-Tac or other quick-setting fabric glue

COMMON LAMPS TURNED CHIC

 amps from discount stores can easily be transformed into something special. Antique white spray paint was used to soften this bright white lamp base, while vintage-style fabric was used to give a new look to an inexpensive cloth shade. Velvet ribbon trim adds a touch of luxury and sweetness at the same time.

1. Use masking tape to protect areas on the lamp base that you don't want to paint. Apply one to two light coats of primer, allowing 20 minutes drying time between coats, then spray paint the lamp base with two or three light coats of antique white paint, allowing 20 minutes drying time between coats. Set aside to dry thoroughly (refer to manufacturer's directions for guidance).

2. Create a template for the lampshade (see "Making Templates," on p. 87).

3. Iron the fabric to remove any wrinkles. Lay the paper template on the right side of the fabric and trace around it with a disappearing-ink pen. Cut outside the trace line on the fabric, leaving ⅜ in. excess on all sides for seam allowance. Fold one edge of the straight seam back along the trace line and iron flat. This will be the overlap for the back seam.

4. Brush a thin, even coat of Yes! paste onto the lampshade with the paste brush.

5. Placing the fabric so it falls on the front of the lampshade, wrap the fabric around the shade, smoothing out any wrinkles or air bubbles with your fingers as you go. If the fabric isn't aligned on your first try, gently pull it up before the glue dries and place on the shade again.

6. Use the small craft paintbrush to add Yes! paste along the back seam of the lampshade; be sure the material is taut, without wrinkles or bubbles, and press the folded edge of the fabric flat with your hand.

7. Cut small slits in the fabric along the top and bottom of the shade, approximately 1 in. apart. Using Yes! paste and the small paintbrush, adhere the fabric to the inside edges of the lampshade.

8. Embellish the lampshade by using Fabri-Tac to attach velvet ribbon around the top and bottom edges. Since any shape of shade other than a drum style has angled edges, the ribbon will need to be cut and pieced together for a smooth finish. Finish by cutting two equal lengths of ribbon (each about 6 in. long) and, holding them together, tie them in a knot (this will give four ribbon tails instead of two). Trim, as desired, and glue it onto the front of the lampshade.

Trade Secret

Many people use spray adhesive when covering a lampshade. It works just fine but its too messy and smelly for my taste. I prefer Yes! paste because it's slow drying (which means you can adjust your fabric if necessary), it can be brushed on very thinly, it dries to a flexible, non-yellowing finish, and it doesn't seep through fabrics.

Is for Mobile

Circus animals cavort under the big top within this fanciful crib mobile made almost entirely of paper. Use the circus critter templates provided or create your own theme for an essential nursery element sure to engage and delight.

TOOLS & MATERIALS

- ✓ Circus Animals and Tent Templates (p. 164)
- ✓ Fine-tipped scissors
- ✓ Patterned scrapbook paper or cardstock, 12-in. by 12-in. sheets, two sheets in complementary designs and colors
- ✓ Extra-strength glue stick
- ✓ Pencil
- ✓ Solid cardstock, 12-in. by 12-in. sheets, six sheets in a variety of complementary colors
- ✓ Black cardstock, one sheet
- ✓ ⅛-in. hole punch
- ✓ Patterned scrapbook or craft paper, scraps for details (optional)
- ✓ Craft glue with a fine-tipped applicator
- ✓ Needle
- ✓ Strong button or coat thread in complementary color
- ✓ 10-in.-dia. wooden embroidery hoop, with exterior ring removed
- ✓ ¼-in. to ½-in. double-sided craft tape

1. Enlarge the Circus Animals and Tent Templates as directed and cut them out along the trace lines.

2. With the wrong sides facing, glue the two pieces of patterned paper together with the glue stick. Trace the Tent Template three times with a pencil onto one side of the patterned paper then cut them out along the trace lines. Erase any visible pencil lines and set aside.

3. Cut two pieces from each sheet of solid cardstock (each piece should be slightly larger than each animal template.) With the wrong sides of each pair of cutouts facing, glue the cutouts together. Again, trace the various animal templates onto the cardstock pieces and cut them out along the trace lines, erasing any stray pencil marks.

4. If desired, add details to the cardstock silhouettes. Use the ⅛-in. hole punch to make eyes from the black cardstock; other embellishments can be cut freehand. Adhere all details using craft glue with the fine-tipped applicator.

5. With the needle, make a small hole in the top of each animal silhouette, using the templates as a guide for placement.

6. Cut six 12-in. lengths of thread and thread one length through the hole in each animal silhouette. Knot the ends and use a dab of craft glue to secure the knot to the silhouette. Loop the other end of the thread around the top of the embroidery hoop a few times and knot. (The animals shown here hang down about 6 in. from the hoop.) Be sure to place the animals around the hoop evenly so that the mobile will balance properly.

7. Once all of the animals have been tied to the embroidery hoop, cut four additional lengths of strong thread for hanging the mobile (thread length will depend on your ceiling height; but as a general rule, cut the thread longer than you think you'll need). Tie a length on each side of the embroidery hoop, forming a cross pattern, then wrap each thread around the hoop a few times and knot the ends. Gather the threads together and loop them around a hook secured in the ceiling or the hanging apparatus of your choice. After securely wrapping the threads around the hanging apparatus, tie them in a knot and trim the excess.

8. Readjust the animals and the hanging threads if needed by gently sliding them along the hoop until the mobile is balanced.

9. After the mobile is balanced and in its proper place, apply double-sided craft tape to the inside edges of the three scalloped tent template cutouts. Secure them to the outside edge of the embroidery hoop, lining up the ends of the three pieces but not overlapping them.

Mobile Safety

All mobiles need to be hung well out of reach of Baby's grasp, and their placement over the crib should be thought of as temporary. When your child is able to stand up in the crib, the mobile will need to be removed or hung in an out-of-the-way place, such as over an armoire or hanging from the ceiling in a corner of the room.

When constructing your mobile, check to make sure all threads are securely knotted on both the cardstock silhouettes and on the embroidery hoop; a dab of craft glue in the hole of each silhouette will give your mobile extra stability.

Is for Night Light

craft map

Night lights in the nursery not only serve as protection from things that go bump in the night but also allow Mom to slip in and out to check on Baby without needing to turn on a bright light. Functionality meets a touch of style with this adorable nursery accent.

TOOLS & MATERIALS

✓ Shade Template (p. 165)

✓ Paper scissors

✓ Night light kit

✓ Scrap of decorative fabric, large enough to cover entire shade

✓ Vellum, 8½-in. by 11-in. sheet

✓ PEELnSTICK double-sided adhesive, 5½ in. by 8¾ in. sheet

✓ Fabric scissors

✓ Pencil

✓ Bone folder (optional)

✓ Strong adhesive, such as Perfect Glue 1

✓ 4 clothespins or other clips

✓ Bias tape, 25 in., in complementary color

✓ Fabri-Tac or other quick-setting fabric glue

FABRIC-COVERED SHADE

 aid the sewing basket for a scrap of fabric to turn what's usually a ho-hum room accessory into a distinctive, decorative accent. Light up the nursery with flare with this quick-and-easy craft project for girls on the go.

1. If you're using the night light kit recommended in Resources, on p. 171, enlarge the Shade Template as directed. Otherwise, enlarge the template to fit the wire frame included in your particular night light kit. (You may have to trim or slightly alter the shape. Check for fit by taping the template to the edges of the wire frame.)

2. Cut one rectangle each from the fabric, vellum, and adhesive sheet, all slightly larger than the shade template. Remove one side of the adhesive backing and adhere the vellum to the adhesive, lining up the edges. Remove the other side of the adhesive backing and adhere the fabric to the adhesive, smoothing out any air bubbles with your fingers or with a bone folder.

3. Lay the shade template over the vellum side of the rectangle and lightly trace around it with a pencil; cut it out along the trace lines and erase any stray pencil marks.

4. Apply a thin line of strong adhesive along the edge of the shade's metal frame. Lay the fabric shade, vellum side down, along the frame and secure each corner with a clothespin or other clip until the glue dries, approximately 1 hour.

5. After the glue has dried, remove the clips and use fabric glue to adhere bias tape along each side of the frame and then over the top and bottom edges, gluing one side of the tape to the edges of the shade and the other side over the metal frame.

Just Your Style

Looking for a more unique approach? Try some of the following materials for covering your night light shade:

- Page from a menu
- Subway map
- Vintage book pages
- Sheet music
- Photograph
- Poem
- Scrapbook paper
- Hole-punched designs in paper
- Dictionary page
- Birth announcement

Some items, such as the menu pages, maps, and scrapbook papers, can be cut and placed directly on the frame. Others, such as photographs and book pages, can be enlarged or reduced, as necessary, and photocopied onto vellum.

TOOLS & MATERIALS

✓ Shade Template (p. 166)

✓ Scissors

✓ Night light kit

✓ Vellum, 8½-in. by 11-in. sheet

✓ PEELnSTICK double-sided adhesive, 5½-in. by 8¾-in. sheet

✓ Pencil

✓ ⅝-in. lightweight seam binding or rayon ribbon, 2 yd. to 3 yd. total, in several complementary colors

✓ Strong adhesive, such as Perfect Glue 1

✓ 4 clothespins or other clips

✓ Bias tape, 25 in., in a complementary color

✓ Fabri-Tac or other quick-setting fabric glue

RIBBON-WRAPPED FRAME

 b anish midnight monsters with this charming yet simple ribbon-wrapped night light. It's quick and easy and a perfect accent for any room.

1. If you're using the night light kit recommended in Resources, on p. 171, enlarge the Shade Template as directed. Otherwise, enlarge the template to fit the wire frame included in your particular night light kit. (You may have to trim or slightly alter the shape.)

2. Cut one rectangle from the vellum and one from the double-sided adhesive; both should be slightly larger than the Shade Template. Remove one side of the adhesive backing and adhere the vellum to the adhesive. Lay the shade template over the vellum side of the rectangle and lightly trace around it with a pencil. Cut it out along the trace lines.

3. Cut the ribbon into 4½-in. lengths. Remove the other side of the adhesive backing and adhere strips of ribbon to the shade, slightly overlapping the edges and working from the center outward. Trim the excess, if necessary.

4. Apply a thin line of strong adhesive along the edge of the metal frame. Lay the fabric shade, vellum side down, along the frame and secure each corner with a clothespin or other clip until the glue dries, approximately 1 hour.

5. After the glue has dried, remove the clips and use fabric glue to adhere bias tape along each side of the frame and then over the top and bottom edges, gluing one side of the tape to the edges of the shade and the other side over the metal frame.

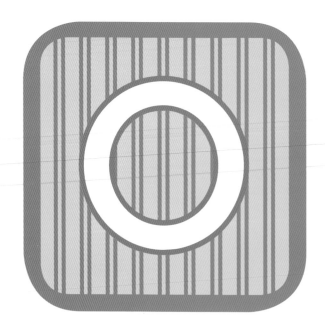

Is for Organizer

New moms can never be too organized! Formerly a shoe storage bag,
this organizer gets a custom touch that adds a colorful lift to the nursery while
keeping things tidy and close at hand.

TOOLS & MATERIALS

- ✓ Printed cotton or canvas fabrics, at least the length and width of the shoe pockets
- ✓ Iron and ironing board
- ✓ Hanging canvas shoe bag with pockets
- ✓ Flexible tape measure
- ✓ Kraft paper for pocket template
- ✓ Pencil
- ✓ Paper scissors
- ✓ Disappearing-ink pen
- ✓ Rotary cutter
- ✓ Cutting mat
- ✓ HeatnBond UltraHold iron-on adhesive sheets (amount depends on the dimensions and number of pockets)
- ✓ Fabri-Tac or other fabric glue
- ✓ Single-fold bias tape (amount depends on the dimensions of the shoe bag)
- ✓ Decorative ribbon (for length needed, multiply the width of the pockets by number of pockets, plus an additional 4 in. for each pocket)
- ✓ Fabric scissors
- ✓ Embellishments, such as buttons and bows (optional)

1. Prewash and dry all fabrics and iron them to remove wrinkles, then iron the pockets on the shoe bag so they are symmetrical and all the creases are smoothed out.

2. Measure the height of the pockets. Then measure the width of the front of the pockets and add 2 in. to that measurement; make note of both measurements. (Usually all the pockets are uniform in size, but if yours differ, you will have to take multiple measurements.)

3. Trace the pocket measurements onto the kraft paper to create a template and cut it out with the scissors. With the disappearing-ink pen, trace the template onto the wrong side of one piece of fabric. Cut around the trace lines with the rotary cutter, leaving a $\frac{1}{2}$-in. seam allowance on all sides. Repeat with the fabric for each pocket.

4. Cut the corners of each piece of fabric on a diagonal (see "Trimming Corners on a Diagonal," on p. 20). Fold in each side $\frac{1}{2}$ in. along the trace lines and iron the folds flat. If desired, add a little fabric glue along the edges to secure.

5. Cut a piece of iron-on adhesive to fit each piece of fabric. Preheat your iron to the silk setting (no steam) and place the adhesive on the wrong side of the fabric, paper side up. Hold the iron on each section of fabric for 2 seconds. Let the fabric cool to the touch then remove the paper. Repeat with all fabric pieces.

6. Attach a fabric piece to each pocket. With your iron still on the silk setting, center the fabric, adhesive side down, on the front of the pocket and fold the excess fabric around the sides of the pocket. Fuse the fabric to the pocket by holding the iron in place for 8 seconds to 10 seconds. Move the iron over the entire surface of the pocket until all the fabric has been fused. Fuse the sides of the fabric in the same way. (If you have difficulty fusing the sides or find it awkward, you can adhere the sides with fabric glue.) Repeat, until all the pockets have been covered.

7. If there are other areas of your organizer that you wish to cover with fabric (such as the top flap of the bag shown at right), make a template with kraft paper by placing it over the desired area and rubbing over the seams with a pencil. Cut out the template along the rubbed outline, check for fit, then trace the template onto the wrong side of the desired fabric. Cut it out around the trace lines, leaving ½ in. for seam allowance on each side, then using the fabric scissors cut slits in the fabric every inch or so down to the pencil line (see "Notching Fabric," on p. 21). Fold the notched fabric in (using the trace lines as a guide) and iron them flat. Attach the fabric with iron-on adhesive as outlined in step 6.

8. For clean-looking seams, use the fabric glue to adhere bias tape around the perimeter of the bag as well as interior areas, such as along the bottoms of the pockets, if desired.

9. Finish each pocket with a length of ribbon glued to the top edge of the pocket. If desired, add additional embellishments such as buttons or bows.

Just Your Style

Most hanging shoe bags have at least 12 pockets, which may seem like too many, depending on where the organizer will be hung. If you'd rather have a smaller bag (like the 9-pocket organizer shown above), simply cut off the bottom row of pockets at the seam where the row of pockets above them ends. The cut will be hidden by the thick seam below the row of pockets; cover the cut with bias tape to finish off the edge.

Is for
Personal Stationery

Personalized stationery makes an excellent gift for a new mom, and the creation of a customized rubber stamp makes it one-of-a-kind. Even better, it's the gift that keeps on giving since Mom can make more when she runs out.

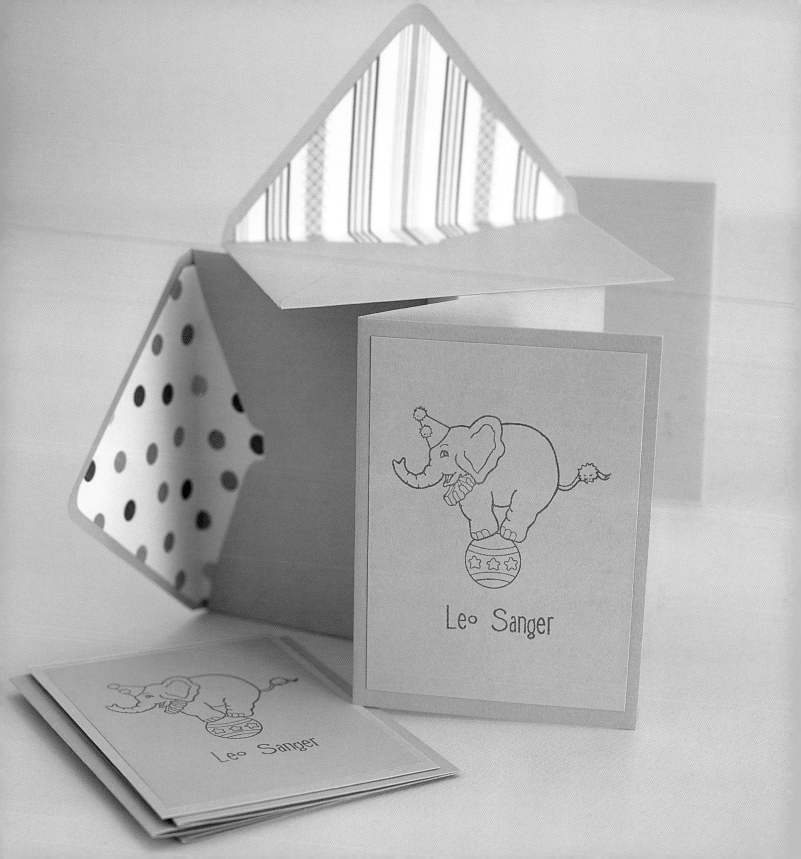

✓ Custom rubber stamp

✓ Computer and printer (optional)

✓ Small note cards or folded cards
(the ones shown measure $3\frac{1}{2}$ in.
by $4\frac{7}{8}$ in.)

✓ Solid text-weight paper,
$8\frac{1}{2}$-in. by 11-in. sheets, in a
complementary color (optional)

✓ Ink pads in complementary
colors

✓ Stamp cleaner

✓ Scissors

✓ All-purpose glue pen or stick

✓ Envelopes corresponding to
card size, plus one extra of the
same size to make envelope
liner template

✓ Cardstock for envelope liner
template

✓ Pencil

✓ Lightweight, decorative paper
for lining envelopes

NOTE CARDS & ENVELOPES

 new addition to the family brings more opportunities for Mom to correspond with friends and family, especially when it comes to thank-you notes. Give her a head start with a customized set of stationery and a personalized rubber stamp that allows her to replenish her note cards when she needs more.

1. To create the custom rubber stamp, first choose a piece of clip art (using a Web site, such as clipart.com, that allows you to download art for personal use for a nominal subscription fee); black and white line art works best. You can also design a monogram on your computer or make your own freehand design with black ink on white paper. Bring the black line drawing or computer printout on white paper to your local office supply store or send it out to a mail-order service specializing in custom rubber stamps (see Resources on p. 172). Stamps are usually ready in a couple of days, and prices vary according to size and complexity.

2. Using your custom rubber stamp, stamp the cards as desired. You can either stamp directly onto your card, or if you're concerned about the proficiency of your rubber stamping, you can stamp onto complementary paper, trim around the best images, and glue them onto the front of the cards. After stamping the cards, clean the rubber stamp with stamp cleaner.

3. To create the envelope liner template, open all the glued edges of the extra envelope so the flaps lay flat on the same plane. Cut off the sides and bottom flaps of the envelope with the scissors and trim the top flap along the line where the glue stops and follow that line down the sides. With a pencil, trace this paper template onto the cardstock and cut it out along the trace lines. This will be your envelope liner template.

4. Trace the envelope liner template onto the wrong side of the decorative paper and cut it out. Slip the liner inside the envelope and fold at the envelope flap. Add a line of glue along the top edges of the liner and secure it to the envelope flap. Repeat with the rest of the envelopes.

Making a Good Impression

Follow these tips to ensure the best stamp impression possible.

- Ink the rubber stamp evenly and press it firmly onto your paper. If your stamp is small, dab it onto the ink pad. If it's large, lay the stamp face up on a hard surface and apply the ink pad to the stamp itself.
- Don't rock the stamp as you're pressing it down; this will blur edges and create unwanted smudges in your image.
- After stamping, lift the rubber stamp in one swift motion, holding the paper down with the other hand.
- Clean your stamps after each use with a commercial stamp cleaner or baby wipes. Baby wipes will help moisturize the rubber (prolonging the life of the stamp), plus they're something every new mother will have on hand.

✓ Computer and printer (optional)

✓ Custom rubber stamp

✓ 67-lb. paper stock for bookplates

✓ Ink pads in desired colors

✓ Stamp cleaner

✓ Ruler

✓ Rotary cutter

✓ Cutting mat

✓ Acid-free glue pen

✓ Ruler

CUSTOM BOOKPLATES

 ustomized bookplates add a special touch to a child's library, especially if you package them with a few classic books to get Baby started.

1. Create a black and white 3-in. by 4-in. bookplate design by hand or compose one with text and clip art on your computer (using a Web site, such as clipart.com, that allows you to download art for personal use for a nominal subscription fee). To make bookplates similar to the ones shown at right, open a blank document in your word-processing program and insert a Text Box that measures 3 in. by 4 in. Use the centering tool and type "This book belongs to" at the top center of the Text Box. Move the cursor down a couple of lines and insert your desired clip art (choose clip art images that are not color dependent; black and white line art works best). Move the cursor below the clip art and type in the child's name. Finish by choosing the type of border with which you want to frame your bookplate design. Test different fonts and sizes to see what fits best within the box and what looks most pleasing to you.

2. Print out the bookplate design on white paper; choose the black and white setting in your print menu. Bring the design to your local office supply store or send it out to a mail-order service

specializing in custom rubber stamps (see Resources on p. 171). Stamps are usually ready in a couple of days, and prices vary according to size and complexity.

3. To make the bookplates, stamp the bookplate design onto heavyweight paper and cut just outside the border with the rotary cutter on the cutting mat, making each of them the same size. After stamping, clean the stamp with stamp cleaner.

Gift Packaging

Note cards & envelopes

Stamp a set of note cards and alternate layers of one card then one envelope; tie a ribbon around the stack. Place the card and envelope stack in a decorative box along with the custom rubber stamp, stamp cleaner, and assorted ink pads.

Custom bookplates

Tie a stack of about 24 bookplates with a ribbon and put them in a decorative box or bag with the rubber stamp, stamp cleaner, ink pads, and an acid-free glue pen for attaching the bookplates. If you're including any books with your gift, attach the bookplates inside the front covers.

Is for Quilted Blanket

Few projects are as time-consuming or satisfying as completing a quilt.
Get a dose of that satisfaction in less time with this simple, quilted patchwork blanket.
It's a sewing-machine version, making it far easier to assemble than a hand-sewn quilt
and requires only a little patience, precision, and imagination.

TOOLS & MATERIALS

- Patterned cotton fabrics of a similar weight, one fat quarter or ¼ yd. to ½ yd. of each fabric (total yardage depends on desired size)
- Woolite
- Iron and ironing board
- Rotary cutter
- Clear acrylic quilter's ruler
- Cutting mat
- Straight pins
- Preshrunk cotton batting (4 in. to 6 in. longer and wider than the blanket dimensions)
- Safety pins
- Sewing machine
- Thread
- ⅞-in. double-fold bias tape in a complementary color
- Cotton flannel for backing in a complementary color (blanket dimensions)

1. Prewash and dry all fabrics and iron them to remove wrinkles.

2. Determine the size blanket you'd like to make and the size you'd like your finished squares to be (the finished squares in the blanket shown are 5 in.). Next, figure out how many squares you will need to achieve the desired blanket dimensions; measure them out on the fabric, then cut them out using the rotary cutter and quilter's ruler on the cutting mat. Be sure to add a ¼-in. seam allowance on all sides of each square (for example, if your finished square is to be 5 in., cut out 5½-in. squares).

3. Arrange the squares on a table or the floor until you've achieved your desired patchwork pattern.

4. Using straight pins and with right sides facing, pin the squares together to form horizontal rows. Sew a ¼-in. seam where one square meets the other. Continue this process until the row is complete, then turn it over and iron all the seams so they lie in one direction. Repeat until each row has been sewn and the seams have been ironed.

5. Pin together the rows of squares; line up the seams precisely, positioning them so all the seams in each row face the same direction. Sew the rows together along the entire length of the row with a ¼-in. seam allowance; iron all the seams in one direction.

6. Spread out the batting, smoothing out any bunches or creases. Lay the patchwork flat on top of the batting and trim the batting around the patchwork, leaving 2 in. to 3 in. on all sides.

7. Beginning in the center of the blanket, pin each patchwork square to the batting with a safety pin (use one pin in the center of each square), smoothing out the layers as you work.

8. Sew the two pieces together by "stitching in the ditch," or sewing directly over each seam. With the patchwork side facing up, start in the center, stitching all the rows in the same direction, from the center outward on that side. Then turn the quilt 45 degrees, and stitch the rows, again working from the center row outward.

9. Trim off the excess batting and remove the safety pins.

10. Add the trim to your blanket. With the patchwork side facing up, place the raw edge of the blanket inside the fold of the bias tape, with the narrower side of the tape facing up. Secure the bias tape around the perimeter of the blanket with straight pins, stretching the tape around the corners.

11. With the rotary cutter, cut the flannel backing to the same size as your blanket. Leave the straight pins in the trim and, with the right sides facing each other, pin the patchwork and the backing together around the perimeter.

12. Sew a ¼-in. seam around the edges of the blanket, making sure to sew through all the layers and leaving 15 in. open on one side. Remove the pins, and turn the blanket inside out. Hand-sew the opening shut, turning the raw edges under and using small stitches to secure the bias tape to the blanket edge.

13. Iron your blanket, using steam.

Trade Secret

To help ensure exact ¼-in. seams on your blanket, place a piece of opaque masking or colored tape on the sewing machine surface ¼ in. from the needle position. The tape is easier to see than most measurement markings on the sewing machine bed, and it will help you feed the fabric in a straight line.

Is for
Reversible Bib

Your baby will love mealtime even more when wearing one of these cheery bibs. Iron-on vinyl makes them durable and wipe-away clean. These bibs are so easy to create, and the sky is the limit with the different colors and patterns you can use to display the range of Baby's personality.

TOOLS & MATERIALS

- ✓ Bib Template (p. 166)
- ✓ Paper scissors
- ✓ Lightweight to medium-weight cotton fabrics, 11-in. by 15-in. pieces, two pieces in complementary prints
- ✓ Therm O Web Iron-on Vinyl in matte or lustre finish, 11-in. by 15-in. pieces, two pieces for each bib
- ✓ Fabric scissors
- ✓ Iron and ironing board
- ✓ Disappearing-ink pen
- ✓ Fabri-Tac fabric glue
- ✓ ¾-in. rickrack, 50 in. per bib, in complementary color
- ✓ Sew-on Velcro® fasteners
- ✓ Needle and thread (optional)

1. Enlarge the Bib Template as directed and make two copies. Cut one along the outer trace line and the other along the inner trace line.

2. Prewash and iron the fabric, then cut the two fabrics a bit larger than the largest template, about 11 in. by 15 in. each.

3. Preheat a dry iron to medium temperature (no steam). Peel one piece of vinyl from its paper and place it sticky-side down on the right side of one piece of fabric, smoothing out any air bubbles with your fingers (line up the edges as accurately as possible).

4. Place the protective paper, from which you peeled the vinyl, shiny side down on top of the vinyl. With medium pressure, hold the iron on one section of the fabric for 8 seconds. Slowly glide the iron over the next area of fabric and again press for 8 seconds. Repeat until the entire vinyl-covered area has been pressed.

5. Turn the piece over, keeping the protective paper on the vinyl covered side, so the uncoated side is up and press each area for 4 seconds until the entire piece of fabric has been pressed. Let the laminated fabric cool to the touch and remove the protective paper. (Set the paper aside for later.)

6. Place the largest bib template on the uncoated side of the laminated fabric and trace around it with the disappearing-ink pen. Cut it out along the trace line.

7. Place the smaller bib template inside the larger fabric cutout and trace around the template with the disappearing-ink pen. Cut small slits from the edge of the bib to the inner trace line approximately every $\frac{1}{2}$ in. along the edge of the bib (see "Notching Fabric," on p. 21). With the uncoated side up and working with one small section at a time, apply Fabri-Tac adhesive along the edge of the bib, folding in the edges along the trace line and lightly pressing with your fingers.

8. Preheat the iron to medium temperature; place the bib, vinyl side up, on the ironing board and cover it with the protective paper (shiny side down). Run the iron over the paper for a few seconds to press the edges of the bib. Let the bib cool and remove the paper.

9. Repeat Steps 3 through 8 with the second piece of fabric.

10. Place one of the bib pieces, uncoated side up, on a flat surface. Working one section at a time, position and glue the rickrack to the bib with the Fabri-Tac. Add more glue to the edge of the second bib piece and place it, uncoated side down, over the rickrack on the first bib piece.

11. Glue the Velcro fasteners to the ends of the bib. If desired, add a hand stitch or two over the Velcro to add durability.

After-Care

For best results, clean your bibs with soap and a damp cloth. If necessary, they can be hand washed in cold water. However, touch up pressing is required after hand washing. When ironing, protective paper or a piece of very smooth fabric must be used between the iron and the laminate, because the warm vinyl surface will easily indent if the surface isn't smooth.

Is for
Storybook Pages

Vintage children's books can provide sweet images to warm your nursery walls.
This version uses scanned pages printed on textured canvas sheets,
so the original books stay intact.

k **K** kitten

TOOLS & MATERIALS

✓ Vintage children's book

✓ Scanner (or book pages scanned and saved to disc)

✓ Computer

✓ Color inkjet printer

✓ 1 package canvas inkjet fabric

✓ Large utility knife

✓ Sturdy mat or illustration board to fit interior of frame

✓ Wooden frame in desired size (no glass)

✓ Decorative fabric or canvas for backing (size depends on frame)

✓ Iron-on fusible web (size depends on frame)

✓ Ruler

✓ Rotary blade

✓ Straightedge

✓ Cutting mat

✓ Iron and ironing board

✓ Fabri-Tac, or other quick-setting fabric glue

✓ Rickrack, about 1 yd.

1. Scan the book pages you wish to frame or have them scanned and saved to a disc at your local copy shop. If necessary, resize the pages to measure 8½ in. by 11 in. or smaller.

2. Place the canvas inkjet fabric face down in your printer; set your printer to print on "best quality" or the comparable setting on your print menu. Print the desired book page and avoid touching the surface of the print for a few minutes until the ink dries.

3. Using the large utility knife, cut the mat or illustration board to fit inside the frame. If your frame already comes with a mat or paper label, use it as a template for sizing your board. If it doesn't, simply measure the space in the back of your frame.

4. Using the rotary cutter, cut a piece of fabric and fusible web ½ in. larger on all sides than the mat board. Following the manufacturer's instructions, adhere the fusible web to the wrong side of the fabric with the iron and then fuse the fabric, web side down, to the front of the mat board. (Follow manufacturer's instructions for fusing time and temperature.)

5. Turn the mat board over and fuse the web-backed fabric to the back of the board, folding in the corners of the fabric first, followed by the long sides, and finishing with the top and bottom edges. Place the board inside the frame.

6. Trim the printed book page, if necessary, and glue it onto the fabric-covered board using the fabric glue. Glue the rickrack around the edges of the print to finish it.

Trade Secret

Trying to fill a large wall space with art that's on the smallish side? Consider a grouping of several framed pages to fill the space. If you're already planning on framing a number of book pages, don't hang them too far apart (1 in. to 2 in. is generally suitable), and measure carefully so the entire group hangs in a level line or square.

Choosing Mats and Frames

The size and style of your frame depend largely on the type of book page that you're framing and the space where you'll hang it. Pairing a large mat and frame with a small piece of artwork can make the artwork look more important. Oversize book pages might require only a 1$\frac{1}{2}$-in. to 2-in. mat, but others may look better with no mat at all. The most important thing is that the frame and mat work together to complement the chosen image, not overwhelm it.

Have your book page in hand when choosing a mat and frame and try it out on a range of frame sizes and types to fully assess the effect of a larger or smaller frame. In addition, try the book page in different layouts—an optically centered page will have a bit more space at the bottom of the mat than at the top; a page with more space on the left or right sides than on the top and bottom creates visual interest.

Ready-made frames are the most cost-effective; plus, because you'll be filling the space with a solid sheet of mat or illustration board, you'll save on the expense of a custom mat.

Is for
Tag Collage

Hanging tags make a perfect vehicle for displaying baby memorabilia that's on the smaller side. Mounted on a simple artist's canvas, the look is contemporary yet the display can be as simple or as ornate as your imagination allows.

TOOLS & MATERIALS

- ✓ 2-in. foam paintbrush
- ✓ Artist canvas, 18-in. by 18-in. piece
- ✓ Small bottle of acrylic craft paint in desired color (for backdrop color)
- ✓ Tag template (p. 167) or 12 hanging tags of similar size
- ✓ Paper scissors
- ✓ Pencil
- ✓ Cardstock for tags in complementary colors
- ✓ ¼-in. hole punch
- ✓ String, about 4 yd.
- ✓ Assorted baby memorabilia and small embellishments
- ✓ Adhesives of your choice (see "Trade Secret," at right)
- ✓ Fabric scissors (optional)
- ✓ Iron and ironing board (optional)
- ✓ Craft glue with a fine-tipped applicator

1. With the foam brush, paint the surface and sides of the artist canvas with two coats of acrylic craft paint, allowing approximately 1 hour drying time between coats.

2. Enlarge the tag template, as directed, and cut it out. Using a pencil, trace the template onto the cardstock 12 times; then cut out the tags along the trace lines.

3. Using the tag template as a guide, punch a hole in the tags, as indicated. (If you are using patterned papers or fabric to cover any of your tags, cover the tags before punching the holes at the top.)

4. Cut a 12-in. string for each tag. Fold a string in half, and insert the loop through the hole in one of the tags, from back to front. Pull the strings extending out the back through the loop extending out the front and pull taut. Repeat for the remaining tags.

Trade Secret

One of the advantages of being a professional crafter is having access to a wide and diverse array of materials, things the average crafter doesn't have. A number of adhesives were used to make the collage shown on p. 125: double-sided adhesive sheets, vellum tape, Perfect Glue, Fabri-Tac, double-sided tape, and regular craft glue. When designing your own collage, take stock of what you're putting on your tags and purchase one or two adhesives that will work best for those items.

5. Decorate and embellish your tags as desired (see "Just Your Style," at right).

6. Lay your painted canvas on a flat surface and arrange the decorated tags until you achieve the layout you desire. Glue each tag to the canvas using the adhesive of your choice (see "Trade Secret," at left). Note that the tags don't need to be fully adhered, just make sure the middle portion of the tag is securely attached to the canvas and leave the edges of the tags glue free.

7. Arrange the strings on the tags as desired and secure the end of each string to the canvas with a dab of craft glue. (Or leave the ends free and apply a dab of glue to the part of the string that naturally lies flat on the canvas.) Allow the glue to dry for 20 minutes to 30 minutes before placing the canvas upright.

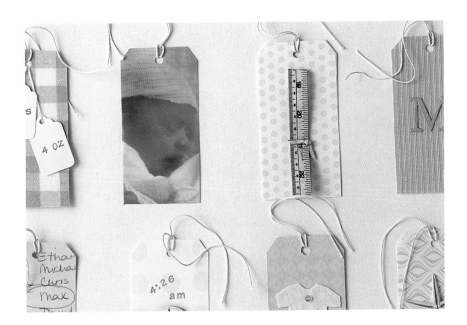

Just Your Style

Not sure what to put on your collage? Use the following list for inspiration; be sure to use color copies of valuable memorabilia that you don't want to cut up. For larger items, such as birth certificates, make reduced-size copies.

- Birth announcements
- First photo
- Footprints or hand prints
- Lock of hair
- Baby spoon
- Sock or bootie
- Birth certificate
- Baby cards
- Hospital bracelet
- Fabric from the receiving blanket
- Fabric from baby's first onesie
- Fabric swatches or paint samples from the nursery
- Monogrammed items
- Tape measure marked with baby's length
- Calendar page with baby's birth date

Is for
Ultrasound

Ultrasound photos are the first glimpse excited parents get of their new baby.
Commemorate those anticipation-filled months with a creatively framed,
archival-quality replica of the images.

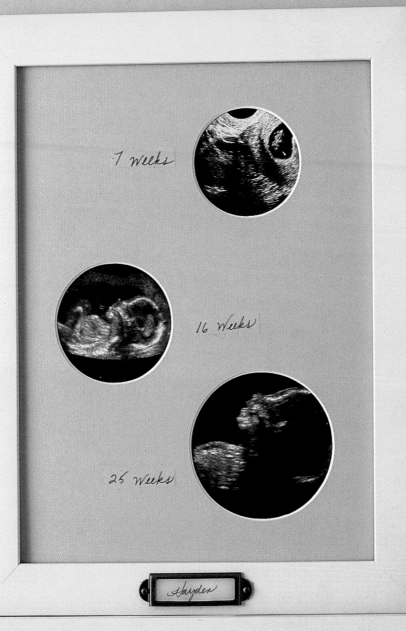

7 weeks

16 weeks

25 weeks

Hayden

TOOLS & MATERIALS

- ✓ Scanner (optional)
- ✓ 3 ultrasound photos from various stages of pregnancy
- ✓ Computer and printer
- ✓ Acid-free white cardstock, 4-in. by 6-in. sheet, three sheets
- ✓ Ultrasound Mat template (p. 167)
- ✓ Mat board in color of your choice, 9-in. by 12-in. piece (available at framing stores)
- ✓ ⅛-in. double-sided tape
- ✓ Vellum, 8½-in. by 11-in. sheet
- ✓ Felt-tipped pen with fine point (optional)
- ✓ Scissors
- ✓ Adhesive tape specially designed for vellum
- ✓ Frame, 9 in. by 12 in.
- ✓ Metal label holder for frame (optional)

1. Scan the ultrasound photos onto your computer or have them professionally scanned and burned to a disc at your local copy shop. Print the scans on acid-free white cardstock. This process will also preserve the quality of your ultrasound photo, because the images on the original photo paper will fade over time.

2. Enlarge the Ultrasound Mat template as directed and bring it to a professional framer. Select the mat board color of your choice and have the framer cut the mat according to the specifications on the template.

3. Back at home, trim each ultrasound copy to slightly larger than the holes in which it will be placed (see "Trade Secret," at right), then place double-sided tape around all the edges on the right side of each ultrasound printout (make sure the tape won't be seen through the holes). With the wrong side of the mat board facing up, tape the earliest ultrasound image in the smallest circle, the midterm ultrasound in the medium circle, and the last ultrasound in the largest circle.

Just Your Style

Another option for personalization is to have a calligrapher write the date and Baby's name directly on the mat.

4. Hand-write the ultrasound dates on the vellum using the felt-tipped pen (or compose them on your computer and print them out onto the vellum). Cut them out, just around the writing, and apply the dates to the mat next to the corresponding photo with the vellum adhesive.

5. Place the completed mat in the frame and, if desired, write Baby's name on the vellum, trim it to size, and place it in a metal label holder, glued or screwed to the bottom of the frame.

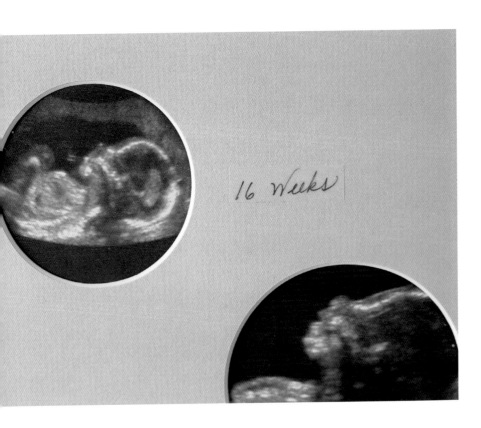

Trade Secret

It's possible that you'll need to adjust the color of your ultrasound scans before printing them on the cardstock, because the ink tones of original ultrasounds are sometimes different from each other. One way to make the printouts uniform in color is to print each ultrasound on the gray scale or black and white setting on your computer's print menu. This will eliminate any color cast that may be present in the scans.

You may also need to resize the ultrasound scans. Not including the background printing around the ultrasound image, you'll need a $2^{3}/_{4}$-in.-dia. image for the smallest opening, a 3-in.-dia. image for the medium opening, and a $3^{5}/_{8}$-in.-dia. image for the largest opening.

Is for
Vintage-Style Frames

Vintage-looking papers and fabrics pay stylistic homage to the past but look fresh and modern when paired with simple, contemporary frames. These frames are so easy to make that you can give or display several to show off the inevitable bounty of baby photos.

✓ Rotary cutter

✓ Cutting mat

✓ Patterned cotton fabric, at least 2¼ in. larger than the frame on all sides

✓ Iron and ironing board

✓ Unfinished wooden frame with a flat front

✓ Pencil

✓ Fabric scissors

✓ Fabri-Tac or other quick-setting fabric glue

✓ Narrow, decorative ribbon for inside of frame (optional)

FABRIC-COVERED FRAME

retro fabrics are all the rage and look especially charming in a nursery setting. The frame featured at right showcases a 1930s-inspired design, a bold and vibrant accent that provides a hefty dose of cheer in a small package.

1. Using the rotary cutter, trim the fabric to measure 2¼ in. larger than the overall frame dimensions.

2. Iron the fabric to remove all wrinkles, and, with the wrong side up, fold in each side ¼ in. and iron flat.

3. With the backing and glass removed, place the frame facedown on the wrong side of the fabric, centering it. Trace around the inside of the frame window onto the fabric with a pencil, then put the frame aside. With scissors, cut a slit in the middle of the fabric to gain access for cutting the center out; then trim the fabric, leaving a ½-in.to ¾-in. seam allowance.Cut slits along the inner cutout, every ½ in. or so, up to the trace line (see "Notching Fabric," on p. 21).

4. Again, place the frame facedown on the wrong side of the fabric,

lining up the trace lines with the frame window. Apply a line of fabric glue around the inside edges of the frame window and bring the fabric through the window to the wood, lining up the notched fabric as neatly as possible and holding it down in the glue.

5. Apply a line of fabric glue to one of the long, outside edges of the fabric, pull it taut (without distorting the pattern), and glue it to the back of the frame. Repeat on the other long side of the fabric.

6. On the short sides of the frame, fold in the ends of the fabric (as if you were wrapping a gift). Apply a line of glue to the short edges and then glue them one side at a time to the back of the frame. Let the glue dry according to the manufacturer's instructions.

7. If desired, finish by gluing decorative ribbon (the same depth as the frame molding) around the inside of the interior frame window.

8. When all the glue is dry, replace the backing and glass and stand the frame upright.

- ✓ Unfinished wooden frame with flat front or flat inset
- ✓ Ruler
- ✓ Scraps of coordinated patterned paper
- ✓ X-Acto® knife or rotary cutter
- ✓ Cutting mat
- ✓ Acrylic craft paint in a complementary color
- ✓ 1-in. foam or bristle paintbrush
- ✓ Decoupage medium in a matte finish (or white craft glue)
- ✓ Damp paper towel or cloth
- ✓ Acrylic spray sealer or varnish in a matte finish (optional)
- ✓ Scrap paper

PATCHWORK-PAPER FRAME

 eminiscent of an old-fashioned quilt, this frame requires nothing more than squares of coordinating paper and a little ribbon to bring it to life. It's the perfect way to use up some of your paper scraps.

1. Remove the frame backing and the glass and measure the length and width of the front of the frame molding and cut enough squares of paper to cover the frame (base the size of your squares on the width of the frame molding).

2. Paint the frame with two coats of acrylic craft paint, allowing 1 hour of drying time between coats. Let the frame dry for an extra hour after the last coat.

3. Once the frame is dry, arrange the paper squares on the front of the frame until the desired layout has been achieved. Remove the squares from the frame and lay them in order next to the frame.

4. Working on one small section at a time, brush a thin layer of decoupage medium or craft glue onto the front of the frame, then place the paper squares on the frame one at a time in the

desired arrangement, with seams just touching. Each time a square is placed, push out any air bubbles with your fingers and wipe off any excess glue with a damp paper towel or cloth while the glue is still wet. Let the frame dry for 30 minutes to 1 hour.

5. After the frame has dried, you can seal it by brushing on one or two light coats of decoupage medium or by spraying the frame with two or three light coats of spray varnish or sealer, following the manufacturer's directions for drying time.

6. Once the frame is dry, replace the backing and glass and stand the frame upright.

- ✓ Unfinished wooden frame with a flat front or flat inset
- ✓ Vintage-style scrapbook paper, 12-in. by 12-in. sheet
- ✓ Pencil
- ✓ Ruler
- ✓ X-Acto knife
- ✓ Cutting mat
- ✓ Scrap paper
- ✓ Fine-grit, spongy emery board (optional)
- ✓ Acrylic craft paint in a complementary color
- ✓ 1-in. foam or bristle paintbrush
- ✓ Decoupage medium in a matte finish (or white craft glue)
- ✓ Damp paper towel or cloth
- ✓ Acrylic spray sealer or varnish in a matte finish (optional)

"VINTAGE" PAPER FRAME

intage-inspired scrapbook papers are readily available in many styles and colors. Paired with a little paint and unfinished frames found at your local craft store, these timeless gems are inexpensive and easy to make.

1. Remove the frame backing and glass and lay the frame facedown on the wrong side of the scrapbook paper. Lightly trace around the exterior and interior of the frame with a pencil and cut out just inside the trace lines with the X-Acto knife on your cutting mat (use the ruler to guide your cuts). (An alternative method is to measure the frame molding and cut the paper to match.)

2. If further aging is desired, place the scrapbook paper right side up on a piece of scrap paper and lightly sand the edges of the scrapbook paper with a fine-grit, spongy emery board (this not only gives an aged look but eliminates any harsh edges on the front of the frame). Set the paper aside.

3. Paint the frame with two coats of acrylic craft paint, allowing 1 hour of drying time between coats. Let the frame dry for an extra hour after the last coat.

4. Brush a thin layer of decoupage medium or craft glue onto the

back of the paper cutout and apply it to the front of the frame, lining up the interior edges of the paper with the frame window. Working from the inside out, smooth out any air bubbles with your fingers until the paper lies flat. Wipe off any excess glue around the edges with a damp paper towel or cloth while the glue is still wet. Let the frame dry for 30 minutes to 1 hour.

5. After the frame has dried, you can seal it by brushing on one or two light coats of the decoupage medium or by spraying the frame with two or three light coats of spray varnish or sealer, following the manufacturer's directions for drying time.

6. Once the frame is dry, replace the backing and glass and stand the frame upright.

Is for Wall Frieze

Inspired by the trendy alphabet flash cards sold to adorn nursery room walls, this homemade version is hip yet timeless. Create your own unique version by tailoring the font and fabric to match the decor of Baby's nursery.

TOOLS & MATERIALS

- ✓ Lightweight assorted cotton fabrics, 2 yd. total, patterns of your choice
- ✓ Iron and ironing board
- ✓ Computer and printer
- ✓ Fine-tipped scissors
- ✓ Rotary cutter with straight blade
- ✓ Cutting mat
- ✓ Fabric scissors
- ✓ Therm O Web HeatnBond UltraHold iron-on adhesive, 17-in. by 5 yd. roll
- ✓ Pencil or ballpoint pen
- ✓ Canvas panels, 6 in. by 8 in., 26 pieces
- ✓ ¼-in. strong, acid-free double-sided tape, 21 yd.
- ✓ Cardstock in a complementary color for finishing, 12-in. by 12-in. sheet, 13 sheets (optional)
- ✓ Craft glue (optional)

1. Prewash all fabrics to remove sizing (this ensures that the adhesive bonds properly and keeps the edges of the fabric from fraying). Iron to remove wrinkles.

2. Pick a font for your project (see "Choosing a Font," below), enlarge the letters on your computer, and print them out. Cut along the lines of the letters to create templates.

3. Cut twenty-six 7-in. by 9-in. pieces of fabric to cover the canvas panels. Arrange the assorted fabrics in your desired pattern (if you're using only two different fabric patterns, simply alternate them). Once the base pattern has been arranged, determine which fabrics you want to make the letters from. Be sure the fabric you choose for each letter cutout has enough contrast so the letter stands out from the base fabric.

4. Cut out pieces for the letter fabrics and cut out iron-on adhesive large enough to cover each letter template. Preheat a dry iron to

Choosing a Font

If you're using lowercase letters, it's best to use fonts that are naturally narrow or use condensed versions of regular fonts. Otherwise, you'll run into trouble fitting wide letters, such as *m* and *w*, and tall letters, such as *b*, *d*, and *f*. The size of individual letters can be adjusted by about 50 points before the difference becomes obvious. The project shown here features the font Garamond BE Condensed at 725 points for the smaller letters and at 675 points for the wider and taller letters (see "Letter Templates," on p. 169).

the silk setting (delicate, no steam). Place the iron-on adhesive, paper side up, on the wrong side of the fabric. Place and hold the heated iron on the paper side of the adhesive for 2 seconds. If necessary, move the iron and repeat until the entire surface is bonded. Allow the fabric to cool to the touch.

5. Place the letter template in reverse on the paper side of the bonded fabric surface. Trace around the letter with the pencil or ballpoint pen and cut out along the lines. Repeat, until all the letters of the alphabet have been made.

6. Cover each canvas panel with a piece of base fabric. With the wrong side of the fabric facing up, place the canvas panel facedown in the center of each piece of fabric. Apply ¼-in. double-sided tape along the back edges of each panel; then remove the paper backing from the tape. Fold the corners of the fabric in first, attaching them to the back of the canvas. Fold the sides in next, pulling the fabric taut, but not distorting the pattern. Finish by folding the top and bottom edges in.

7. Preheat the iron to the silk setting. Starting with the first letter, peel the paper backing off of the letter and place it in the desired location on the canvas panel. With the panel on an ironing board, iron over the letter for 8 seconds to 10 seconds or until the letter is completely bonded. Repeat until all alphabet cards are complete.

8. To neatly finish the back, cut cardstock into 26 pieces (5½ in. by 7½ in.). Attach cardstock to each alphabet card with double-sided tape or craft glue.

Hanging the Alphabet Cards

An easy and great-looking way to display your alphabet cards on the nursery wall is to nail two parallel strips of panel molding, the same length as your finished cards, to the wall. Space the strips ½ in. closer together than the actual height of the cards. To insert, bend the cards slightly and pop the ends in under the strips.

Is for
Xtra Storage

There's rarely enough storage in the nursery, a situation easily remedied with hatboxes, which serve a decorative purpose as well. Covered with scrubbable wallpaper, these storage gems are a great way to use leftovers from a home project.

TOOLS & MATERIALS

✓ Round papier-mâché hatboxes in graduated sizes (the largest one shown here has a 13-in. dia.)

✓ Tape measure

✓ Prepasted wallpaper remnants (must be large enough to cover the boxes)

✓ Rotary cutter

✓ Cutting mat

✓ Ruler

✓ Shallow dish or basin for water

✓ 2-in. bristle or foam paintbrush

✓ Scissors

✓ Pencil

✓ Thin, decorative ribbon, enough to circle each box twice (optional)

✓ Fabri-Tac or other quick-setting fabric glue (optional)

1. Measure the height and circumference of each hatbox base (you'll measure the lid later), adding 1/2 in. to the total circumference of the box and 2 in. to the height. Make note of your measurements.

2. Using the rotary cutter, the ruler, and the cutting mat, trim the wallpaper to the measurements calculated in Step 1.

3. Fill the shallow dish with warm water (you may need to change the water several times throughout this project as the water cools off). Brush a light coat of warm water onto the backside of the wallpaper, leaving approximately 1 in. dry along the long edges of the wallpaper, at the top and bottom. Let it sit for 1 minute to 2 minutes; this allows the adhesive on the wallpaper to soften, giving it more flexibility.

4. Start by determining where you will place the back seam then wrap the wallpaper around the base of the hatbox, smoothing out air bubbles with your fingers as you go. When you are finished, the back seams will overlap by 1/2 in. and there will be a 1-in. extension of paper along the top and bottom edges of the box.

5. Use the scissors to notch the paper down to the box edge (see "Notching Fabric," on p. 21) approximately every inch around the box, both on the top and on the bottom.

6. Brush a light coating of water onto the top notched border, let it sit for 1 minute to 2 minutes, then fold in the edges and adhere them to the inside of the box, lining up the notched edges as best

you can. Repeat along the bottom border, adhering the notches to the bottom of the box.

7. With a pencil, lightly trace around the bottom of the hatbox onto the wrong side of more wallpaper. Use scissors to cut out the circle along the trace line. Brush water onto the back of the wallpaper, letting it sit as before, then adhere it to the bottom of the hatbox.

8. Trace around the lid onto the wrong side of another piece of wallpaper, then trim around the circle, leaving a $1/2$-in. overhang around the entire perimeter. Notch the outer edges of the circle to the penciled line every inch or so. Brush water onto the entire cutout, let it sit, then apply it to the top of the lid, lining up the lid inside the penciled circle. Apply more water to the notches if they become dry, and smooth the notched edges along the sides of the lid.

9. Measure the height and circumference of the lid, then cut a strip of wallpaper to that measurement. Brush water onto the strip, let it sit, and apply it around the sides of the box lid, covering the notched paper. (If your lid is loose enough, you can cut the strip of paper with a $1/2$-in. overhang, notch the extending paper to the lid's edge, and bring the paper over the sides of the box lid and adhere the notches to the interior.)

10. If desired, finish the hatbox by applying ribbon to the top and bottom edges of the lid with Fabri-Tac.

Trade Secret

To cover the interior of a box with wallpaper, cut circles for the interior of the base and lid, just a bit larger than the corresponding exterior dimensions. Notch the edges. Cut strips of wallpaper to the height and circumference of the base and lid and attach them to the interior sides of the base and lid, covering the notched edges of the circles. Another alternative is simply to paint the interiors with acrylic craft paint in a complementary color.

Is for Your Name

Expectant parents generally put a great deal of energy into finding the perfect name for their new baby. Celebrate this important decision with a nursery accessory that spells it out.

✓ Complementary patterned cotton fabrics, ½ yd. of each (½ yd. yields two to three letters)

✓ Iron and ironing board

✓ 12-in. papier-mâché letters

✓ Disappearing-ink pen

✓ Fabric scissors

✓ Cotton batting, approximately 5-in. by 12-in. piece for each letter

✓ Fabri-Tac or other quick-setting fabric glue

✓ Flexible tape measure

PADDED PAPER-MÂCHÉ LETTERS

pruce up purchased papier-mâché letters with patterned fabric and a little cotton batting. Use their three-dimensional nature to your advantage by displaying them on a shelf, dresser, or deep window ledge.

1. Iron the fabric to remove any wrinkles. Place each of the papier-mâché letters on the wrong side of the fabric and trace around them with the disappearing-ink pen. Make two tracings for each letter, one for the front side of the letter and one for the back side.

2. Cut around the trace lines on the fabric, approximately ½ in. outside the lines. Cut small slits all around the edges to the trace line, about every ½ in. or so (see "Notching Fabric," on p. 21), and set the fabric aside.

3. Lay each papier-mâché letter facedown on top of the batting and trace around each with the disappearing-ink pen. Cut them out on the trace lines.

4. Glue the batting cutouts to the surface of each papier-mâché letter using fabric glue. Trim any excess batting from the edges if necessary (see "Padding Letters," on p. 21).

5. Lay one batting-covered letter, batting side down, on the wrong side of its corresponding fabric cutout, lining up the letter within the traced outline on the fabric. Apply a line of fabric glue to the edges of the notched fabric and glue them to the sides of the papier-mâché letter (see "Notching Fabric," on p. 21). Continue until all of the fabric has been adhered to each letter.

6. Lay the reverse side of the papier-mâché letter on the wrong side of the second piece of fabric prepared for it, again lining up the papier-mâché with the traced outline. Apply fabric glue to the notched edges of the fabric and adhere them to the sides of the letter as before.

7. Measure around the letter with the tape measure and cut a strip of fabric approximately 2 in. wide by the length of the letter measurement. (Cut additional 2-in.-wide strips for the interior of certain letters, such as the letter A.) Fold in one long edge of the fabric approximately ½ in. and iron flat. Repeat on the other side, again folding in the long edge approximately ½ in.

8. Glue the fabric strips around the sides of the letter, joining the ends in the least obvious area. Trim the end so it doesn't overlap, if necessary.

9. Repeat Steps 5 through 8 for each remaining letter.

TOOLS & MATERIALS

- ✓ Computer and printer or copier

- ✓ White computer or copier paper, 8½-in. by 11-in. sheets (one sheet yields one letter)

- ✓ Paper scissors

- ✓ PEELnSTICK double-sided adhesive, 11-in. by 17-in. sheets (one sheet yields about two letters)

- ✓ Heavy white cardstock, 8½-in. by 11-in. sheet (one sheet yields one letter)

- ✓ Complementary fabrics, 8½-in. by 11-in. pieces (one piece yields one letter)

- ✓ Pencil

- ✓ Fabric scissors

- ✓ ½-in.-wide ribbon

- ✓ Craft glue

- ✓ 2 thumbtacks

- ✓ 2 decorative buttons (optional)

HANGING NAME

t is easy and fun to create this decorative wall hanging for the nursery. If you're not interested in working with fabric, use patterned papers or wallpaper remnants to create your own version, following the same easy steps outlined here.

1. Choose a font to create Baby's name and enlarge each letter to the desired size. (The example here features lowercase letters from the B Americana Bold font; see "Letter Templates," on p. 169.) Print out the letters and cut them out along the trace lines to create the templates.

2. Cut out rectangles of double-sided adhesive slightly larger than each letter. Remove the paper side of the adhesive and apply it to the cardstock. Trim the cardstock to the same size as the adhesive. Repeat with one piece of cardstock for each letter.

3. Remove the shiny side of the adhesive sheets and adhere the fabric pieces to the exposed adhesive.

4. Turn one piece of cardstock over and place one letter template on it in reverse position. Trace around the letter with a pencil and cut it out along the trace lines. Repeat for each letter.

5. Make ribbon loops for hanging the letters. With the width of your ribbon as a guide, make loops of ribbon just wide enough for another piece of ribbon to pass through. Glue the ends of the ribbon together to form the loops. (Some letters, such as *i* and *l* will only need one loop; others, such as *m* and *w* will need two loops of ribbon per letter for balance when hung.) Glue the loops to the backs of each letter, aligning each set of loops so the ribbon length will be consistent when hung. (See "Making Loops for Hanging" on p. 21.)

6. Once the loops are dry and secure and the letters are in order, pass a piece of uncut ribbon through them, starting with the first letter of Baby's name. When all the letters have been strung, space them out as desired by sliding them along the ribbon. Determine how much ribbon you'd like to have on each end, then trim the ribbon to size.

7. Tack the ends of the ribbon onto the wall. Make bows from another length of ribbon, if desired, and glue them over the tacks to hide them or glue a decorative button over each tack instead of ribbon, if desired.

Just Your Style

Purchase wooden letters from your local craft store, then paint them and stamp patterns on them with rubber stamps. See p. 68 for techniques on painting and stamping wood.

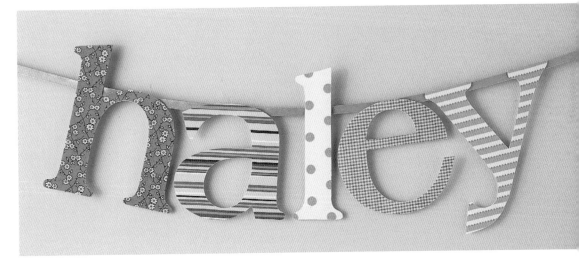

Is for Zoo Animals

Stimulate Baby's imagination and senses with colorful, whimsical zoo animals ironed on canvas and bound into a book. This first book for Baby is durable, child friendly, and washable.

TOOLS & MATERIALS

- ✓ Zoo Animal Templates (p. 168)
- ✓ Letter templates (p. 169)
- ✓ Opaque canvas fabric, ½ yd.
- ✓ Patterned cotton fabric scraps, large enough to cover the animal templates
- ✓ Iron and ironing board
- ✓ Rotary cutter
- ✓ Cutting mat
- ✓ Sewing machine
- ✓ Thread
- ✓ Fray Check® or FrayBlock® (optional)
- ✓ Ruler
- ✓ Disappearing-ink pen
- ✓ Therm O Web Heatnbond UltraHold iron-on adhesive
- ✓ Paper scissors
- ✓ Pencil
- ✓ Fabric scissors
- ✓ Felt scraps (optional)
- ✓ Black or brown textile marker (optional)
- ✓ ¹⁄₁₆-in. hole punch (optional)
- ✓ Craft glue with fine-tipped applicator (optional)

1. Enlarge the Zoo Animal Templates as directed and cut them out. Enlarge the appropriate letters choosing from the "Letter Templates" on pp. 169–170, so they measure approximately 7 in. wide.

2. Prewash, dry, and iron canvas and fabrics to remove wrinkles.

3. Using the rotary cutter and the cutting mat, trim the canvas into three 8-in. by 16-in. rectangles.

4. With the sewing machine, reinforce the perimeter of the canvas rectangles with a zigzag stitch (or use Fray Check or FrayBlock along the edges). Stack the canvas rectangles together, aligning them the best you can, and fold the stack in half so the shorter edges meet; press the fold with an iron, forming the book's pages. Open the pages and line up the ruler with the fold line. Trace over the line with the disappearing-ink pen, and sew a straight stitch down the center of the book, following the trace line.

5. Cut the fabric scraps and the HeatnBond iron-on adhesive into pieces slightly larger than each animal and letter template. Set the iron to the silk setting (dry, no steam). With the fabric wrong side up, place the adhesive shiny side down onto the fabric. Hold the iron over the adhesive sheet for 2 seconds, moving the iron and pressing in sections until the entire piece of fabric has been pressed. Repeat with each piece of fabric.

6. Place the animal and letter templates in reverse on the papered sides of the fabric scraps and trace around them with a pencil. Cut them out along the trace lines with fabric scissors.

7. When all the templates have been traced onto the fabric and cut out, add details as desired (eyes, nose, etc.) using felt, different patterned fabric, or a textile marker. The templates provide some ideas for where to place the details.

8. Arrange the letters and animals as desired on the pages. Once the layout has been determined, remove the paper backing from the fabric cutouts, place them as desired on the page, and hold a dry iron, set to the silk setting, over the cutouts for 8 seconds to 10 seconds each. (Some fabrics may require slightly longer bonding time.) Repeat, until all the pages have been completed.

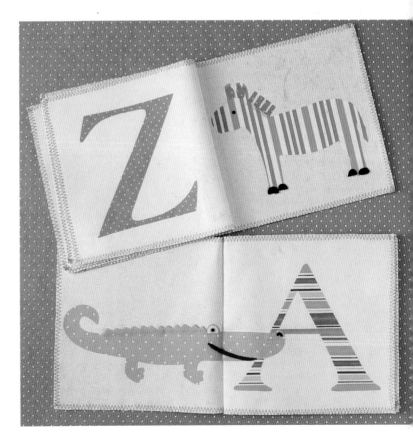

Diaper Announcement

Enlarge by 200%

Card for Diaper Announcement

Enlarge by 125%

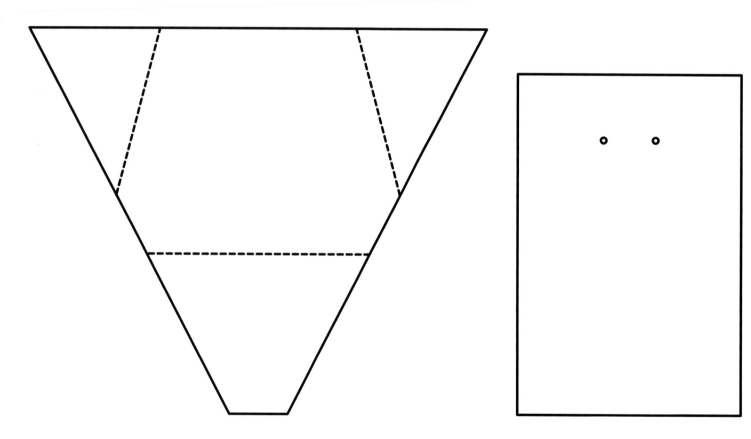

Is for Customized Disc

CD Package

Enlarge by 155%

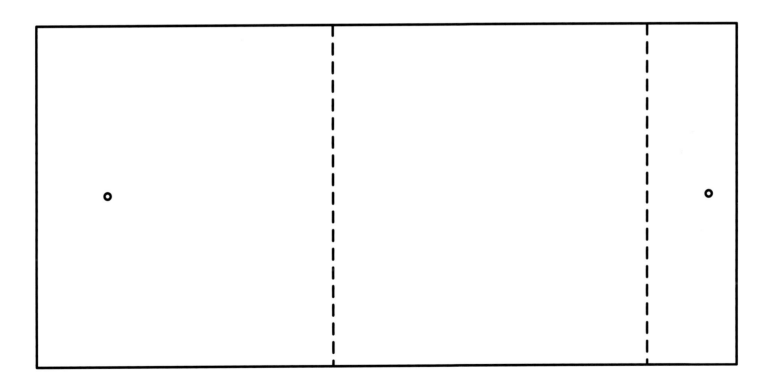

Is for Decoupage

Bath Bucket Top & Bottom

Enlarge by 155%

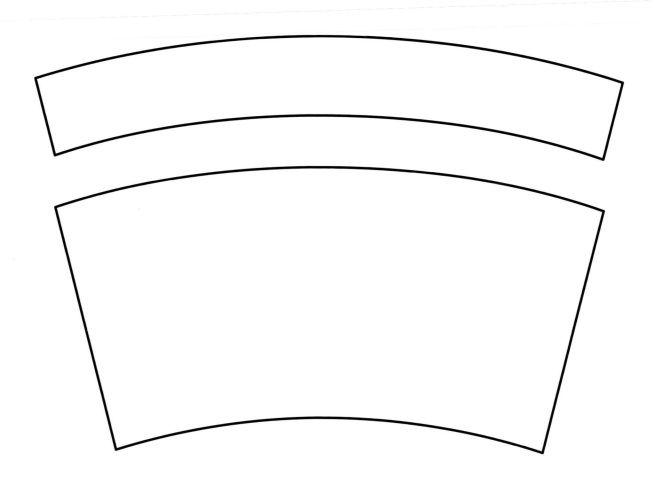

Onesie Appliqués

Enlarge by 155%

Shoe Templates don't come with enlargement templates since foot sizes will vary—see directions for shoes in "F".

Sole

Shoe Template #2   Strap

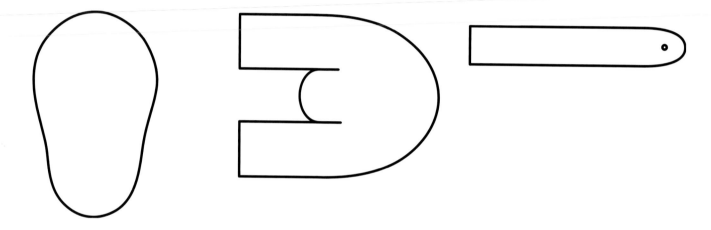

Shoe Template #1   Shoe panel

Flowers

Actual size

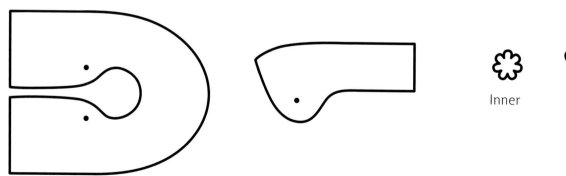

Inner

Outer

Is for Growth Chart

Giraffe

Enlarge by 725%

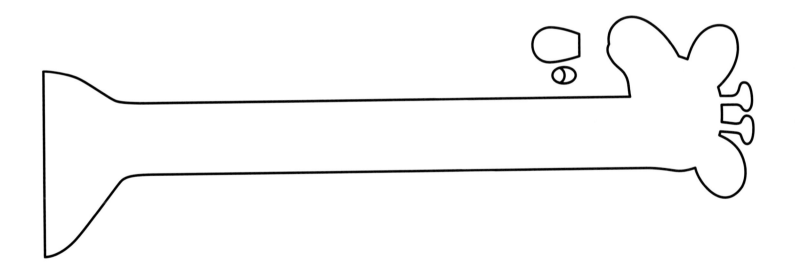

Tent

Enlarge by 200%

Circus Animals

Enlarge by 250%

Shade

Enlarge by 120%

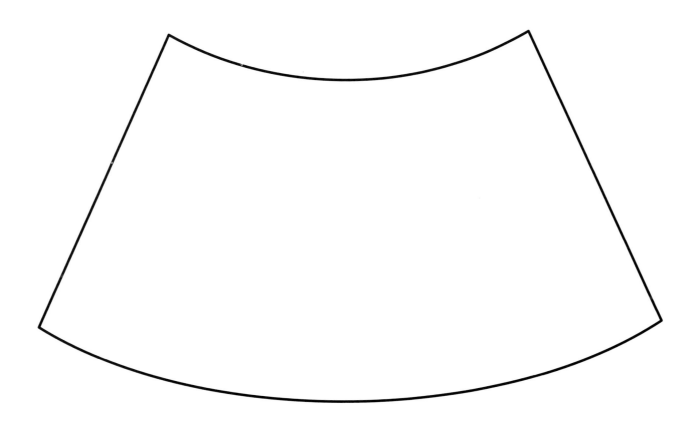

R Is for Reversible Bib

Bib

Enlarge by 245%

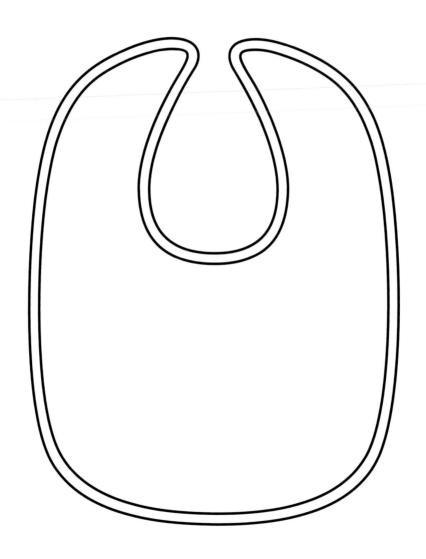

T
Is for Tag Collage

U
Is for Ultrasound

Tag

Enlarge by 110%

Ultrasound Mat

Enlarge by 250%

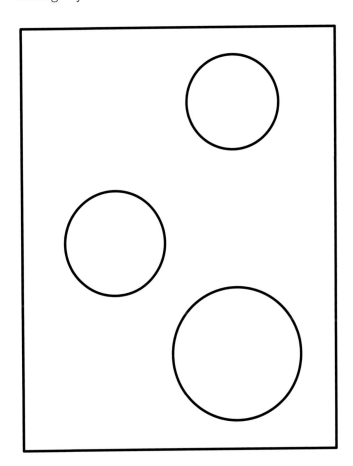

Z Is for Zoo Animals

Zoo Animals

Enlarge by 285%

Letter Templates

a b c d e f g h i j k l m

n o p q r s t u v w x y z

A B C D E F G H J K

L M N O P Q R S T U

V W X Y Z

Letter
Templates

a b c d e f g h i j k l m n
o p q r s t u v w x y z

A B C D E F G H I J K
L M N O P Q R S T U
V W X Y Z

Resources

The following is a list of resources for the products used in this book. I've also included a few of my favorite stores and online sites—places you're always sure to find something useful, fun, or inspirational for craft projects.

B&J Fabrics
525 Seventh Avenue
2nd Floor
New York, NY 10018
212-354-8150
Large selection of patterned cotton fabrics

Beacon Adhesives
www.beaconcreates.com
914-699-3405
Product info for Fabri-Tac

Belton Molotow Premium Spray Paint
www.shopbelton.com
213-741-0097
High-quality spray paint in unusual colors

Britex Fabrics
146 Geary Street
San Francisco, CA 94108
www.britexfabrics.com
415-392-2910
Fabric, trim, buttons, ribbons, flowers, and appliqués

Chatterbox, Inc.
www.chatterboxinc.com
888-416-6260
Coordinated scrapbook papers and embellishments

Clipart.com
www.clipart.com
800-482-4567
Subscription-based clip art service (1 week subscriptions available)

The Craft Pedlars, Inc.
www.pedlars.com
877-733-5277
Papier-mâché boxes, alphabet letters

Create for Less
www.createforless.com
866-333-4463
Excellent discount source, especially for Therm O Web products

Daytona Trimming
251 West Thirty-ninth Street
New York, NY 10018
212-354-1713
Large selection of rickrack, bias tape, and decorative trim

DCC Crafts
www.dcccrafts.com
316-685-6265 ext. 015
Large selection of papier-mâché

Dick Blick
www.dickblick.com
800-828-4548
General art supplies and tools

Equilter.com
www.equilter.com
877-FABRIC-3
Huge selection of patterned cotton fabrics

Fiskars
www.fiskarscrafts.com
866-348-5661
All types of scissors, rotary cutters, cutting mats, hole punches

Hangers.com
www.hangers.com
800-400-6680
Wooden infant and children's hangers

Impress Rubber Stamps
www.impressrubberstamps.com
206-901-9101
Blank matchboxes, paper crafting supplies, tools, rubber stamps, ink pads

Jamali
www.jamaligarden.com
212-244-4025
Galvanized tin buckets

Jo-Ann Stores
www.joann.com
888-739-4120
Craft and sewing supplies, fabric

Kate's Paperie
www.katespaperie.com
800-809-9880
Extensive selection of papers in their retail stores

The Lamp Shop
www.lampshop.com
603-224-1603
Night light kits, lamp shades and supplies

M&J Trimming
1008 Sixth Avenue
New York, NY 10018
www.mjtrim.com
800-9-MJTRIM
Ribbon, trim, buttons, and buckles

Magic Cabin Dolls
www.magiccabindolls.com
888-623-3655
Extensive selection of wool felt, sold in small amounts

Making Memories
www.makingmemories.com
801-294-0430
Scrapbook supplies, paper sewing kit

New York Central Art Supply
62 Third Avenue
New York, NY 10003
www.nycentralart.com
800-950-6111
General art supplies, extensive collection of artist and drawing papers

Paper Presentation
23 West Eighteenth Street
New York, NY 10011
www.paperpresentation.com
800-727-3701
Scrapbook papers and supplies, extensive
selection of artist papers and stationary

Paper Source
www.paper-source.com
888-PAPER-11
Wonderful papers and paper crafting supplies,
stationary, bookbinding supplies and tools

Pearl Paint
www.pearlpaint.com
800-451-7327
General art supplies and tools

Perfect Glue
www.perfectglue.com
866-321-4583
Product info, where to buy, craft projects

Plaid
www.plaidonline.com
800-842-4197
Mod Podge, acrylic paints and other craft
supplies

Print Icon
7 West Eighteenth
New York, NY 10011
www.printicon.com
212-255-4489
Decorative papers

Rosen & Chadick
561 Seventh Avenue
2nd and 3rd Floors
New York, NY 10018
212-869-0142
Large selection of patterned cotton fabrics

Stampworx 2000
212-679-5370
Custom rubber stamps

Staples
www.staples.com
Iron-on transfer paper

Therm O Web
www.thermoweb.com
847-520-5200
Product info, where to buy, craft projects

Tinsel Trading Company
47 West Thirty-eighth Street
New York, NY 10018
www.tinseltrading.com
212-730-1030
A treasure trove of vintage trim, millinery
flowers, other unique items

Tsukineko
www.tsukineko.com
800-769-6633
StazOn solvent ink pads as well as pigment ink
pads

The Store across the Street (also owned by
Tinsel Trading)
64 West Thirty-eighth Street
New York, NY 10018
www.tinseltrading.com
212-354-1242
Specializing in contemporary and vintage ribbon

Sure Thing
www.surething.com
800-998-4555
CD labeler software, labels

The Vintage Workshop
www.thevintageworkshop.com
913-341-5559
Inkjet canvas fabric sheets, extensive collection
of downloadable vintage images

Specific Project Resources

A Is for Announcements
Diaper: tangerine gingham paper by
Chatterbox, Inc.
Matchbox: slider boxes by Impress Rubber
Stamps; decorative papers from Paper
Source
Footprint: plaid paper from Print Icon; "Luxe
Glass" paper lining envelope from Paper
Source; decorative ribbon from Making
Memories

C Is for Customized Discs
All patterned cardstock from Making
Memories; Sure Thing CD labeling software

D Is for Decoupage
Personalized stool: patterned paper from
Making Memories; rickrack from Daytona
Trimming
Bath bucket: patterned papers from
Chatterbox, Inc.; galvanized bucket from

Jamali; spray paint for interior of bucket
by Belton

F Is for Felt Shoes
All wool felt from Magic Cabin Dolls

G Is for Growth Chart
Rub-on transfer numbers by Making
Memories

H Is for Hangers
Hangers from IKEA; all spray paint by Belton;
Dot rubber stamp from Impress Rubber
Stamps; Vintage Hip paper collection from
Making Memories

I Is for Iron-on Transfer
Iron-on transfer paper by Avery; rickrack
from Daytona Trimming

J Is for Journals
Bookboard and polka dotted paper from
Paper Source; drawing paper (for accordion
folded pages) from New York Central Art
Supply; metal label holder and rub-on
transfer letter from Making Memories

L Is for Lampshades
All vintage lamp bases purchased on eBay; all
lampshades and modern lamp base from
Target

P is for Personal Stationary
Circus set: plain stationary and solid paper
from Paper Source; papers lining envelopes
from Chatterbox, Inc; clip art from
Jupiterimages, Clipart.com; custom stamp
from Stampworx 2000
Monogrammed: plain cards and envelopes
from Kate's Paperie; papers lining
envelopes from Anna Griffin; custom stamp
from Stampworx 2000
Bookplates: clip art image from
Jupiterimages, Clipart.com; custom stamp
from Stampworx 2000

S Is for Storybook Pages
ABC Picture Book by Florence Salter, 1942,
Merrill Publishing Company

Q Is for Quilted Blanket
Double-fold bias tape from Jo-Ann stores

X Is for Xtra Storage
Wallpaper from Cath Kidston